UNHAPPY UNION

OTHER ECONOMIST BOOKS

Guide to Analysing Companies
Guide to Business Modelling
Guide to Business Planning
Guide to Cash Management
Guide to Commodities
Guide to Decision Making
Guide to Economic Indicators
Guide to Emerging Markets
Guide to the European Union
Guide to Financial Management
Guide to Financial Markets
Guide to Hedge Funds
Guide to Investment Strategy
Guide to Management Ideas and Gurus
Guide to Managing Growth
Guide to Organisation Design
Guide to Project Management
Guide to Supply Chain Management
Numbers Guide
Style Guide

Book of Business Quotations
Book of Isms
Book of Obituaries
Brands and Branding
Business Consulting
Business Strategy
Buying Professional Services
Doing Business in China
Economics
Managing Talent
Managing Uncertainty
Marketing
Marketing for Growth
Megachange – the world in 2050
Modern Warfare, Intelligence and Deterrence
Organisation Culture
Successful Strategy Execution
The World of Business

Directors: an A–Z Guide
Economics: an A–Z Guide
Investment: an A–Z Guide
Negotiation: an A–Z Guide

Pocket World in Figures

UNHAPPY UNION

How the euro crisis – and Europe –
can be fixed

John Peet and **Anton La Guardia**

THE ECONOMIST IN ASSOCIATION WITH
PROFILE BOOKS LTD

Published by Profile Books Ltd
3a Exmouth House
Pine Street
London EC1R 0JH
www.profilebooks.com

Typeset in EcoType by MacGuru Ltd
info@macguru.org.uk

Printed in Great Britain by Clays, Bungay, Suffolk

A CIP catalogue record for this book is available from the British Library

Hardback ISBN: 978 1 78125 291 8
Paperback ISBN: 978 1 78125 292 5
e-book ISBN: 978 1 78283 083 2

Contents

List of figures

Acknowledgements

MANY POLITICIANS, OFFICIALS, diplomats, academics, think-tankers and fellow journalists have helped us to form our ideas and write this book, some without realising it. A large number of people gave generously of their time and shared their insights (and often their personal notes of events), but wish to remain anonymous. We would like to thank them all.

For the Charlemagne columnist covering the twists and turns of the crisis from Brussels, the press corps has been a source of good cheer and comradeship, and a forum for the exchange of information, through endless late-night meetings of European leaders and finance ministers. The colleagues and guests of the "Toucan" dinner club have produced many enlightening and enjoyable evenings.

The job of interpreting events has been made much easier thanks to the expertise of scholars who follow the often arcane affairs of the EU. They include staff at the Brussels think-tank, Bruegel – among them Guntram Wolff, Jean Pisani-Ferry, André Sapir, Zsolt Darvas and Silvia Merler – who have offered invaluable expertise over the years. Similarly, Daniel Gros at the Centre for European Policy Studies has been a source of sharp perspective. On questions of Europe in the wider world many have been helpful and incisive, among them Jan Techau at Carnegie Europe, Daniel Keohane at FRIDE, Sir Michael Leigh at the German Marshall Fund of the United States, as well as the many experts of the European Council on Foreign Relations. Philippe Legrain, formerly at the European Commission's Bureau of European Policy Advisers, has been refreshingly trenchant and forthright in his views of where Europe has gone wrong.

We would like to thank Stephen Brough, Penny Williams and

Jonathan Harley for incubating this book and seeing it through to completion with charm and patience, despite many interruptions and changes to the manuscript. Andrea Burgess and Roxana Willis at *The Economist* have been indefatigable researchers in finding data and producing charts.

We owe a special thanks to several people who took the time to read drafts of our manuscript and commented on all or parts of it. They include Charles Grant and Simon Tilford at the Centre for European Reform and Heather Grabbe at the Open Society Foundations, as well as our colleagues at *The Economist*, Edward Carr and Zanny Minton Beddoes.

No one can write a book without being a burden on their families. Accordingly, we dedicate this one to our ever-supportive spouses, Sara and Jane.

Preface

EUROPE HAS LONG PRIDED ITSELF on being a model for the rest of the world of how to reconcile old enemies after centuries of war, blend the power of capitalism with social justice and balance work with leisure. Little matter that Europeans did not generate as much wealth as overworked Americans; Europeans took more time off to enjoy life. And little matter that Europe could not project the same military force as the United States; Europe saw itself as a "normative power", able to influence the world through its ability to set rules and standards. Some Europhiles even imagined that Europe would "run the 21st century", as the title of one optimistic book put it.[1]

The collapse of subprime mortgages in the United States, and the credit crunch that followed, only confirmed such convictions. The single currency, the European Union's most ambitious project, was seen as a shield against financial turbulence caused by runaway American "ultra-liberalism", as the French liked to describe the faith in free markets. But when the financial storm blew in from across the Atlantic, the euro turned out to be a flimsy umbrella that flopped over in the wind and dragged away many of the weaker economies. It led to the worst economic and political crisis in Europe since the second world war.

Starting in May 2010, first Greece, then Ireland and Portugal were rescued and had to undergo painful internal devaluation, that is, by reducing wages and prices relative to others. The process proved so messy and bitter that, even with hundreds of billions of euros committed to bail-outs, the currency several times came close to breaking up, potentially taking down the single market and perhaps the whole EU with it. The EU's hope of becoming a global power dissolved as Europe became the world's basket case. More than once, the United States forcibly pressed its transatlantic allies and economic partners to do more to fix their flawed currency union.

At the time of writing, in March 2014, the euro zone has survived the financial crisis – an achievement in itself, but won at too high a price. The euro zone bottomed out of its double-dip recession in 2013. But despite signs of "Europhoria" in markets the danger is far from over.

Among Europhiles and Eurosceptics alike, there is a growing belief that the euro has undermined, and may yet destroy, the European Union. Instead of promoting economic integration, euro-zone economies have diverged. Rather than sealing post-war reconciliation, the euro is creating resentment between north and south. Far from settling the age-old German question, Germany has emerged as all-powerful. The decline of France has accelerated, and the ungovernability of Italy has been reaffirmed. Tensions between euro "ins" and "outs" have increased, particularly in the case of the UK, which now hovers ever closer to the exit.

The chronic democratic problem has become acute: the EU is intruding ever more deeply into national policymaking, particularly in the euro zone, without becoming any more accountable to citizens. Perversely, the clearest sign of a common political identity, the European "demos" that federalists hoped would emerge, is to be found in anti-European movements.

For now the riots and clouds of tear gas in Greece and the mass protests by Spain's *indignados* may have faded away. But almost everywhere, apart from Germany, which has barely felt the crisis, indignant voters have thrown out incumbent governments and abandoned centrist parties in large numbers. Anti-EU and anti-euro parties are on the rise, of both left- and right-wing varieties, in both core and periphery countries, and in both euro ins and euro outs. The scariest are in Greece, which has both radical leftists and neo-Nazi extremists, and has witnessed murderous violence among their followers. But the most consequential may yet be the scrubbed-up, besuited populists in countries such as France, the Netherlands and the UK, which were hardly the worst hit by the debt crisis. They have already changed the terms of the European debate in these countries. Once the champion of EU enlargement, the UK is increasingly turning against the cherished right of free movement of workers, and against the EU itself.

As the countries of the euro-zone periphery seek to regain competitiveness, their most striking export has been young emigrants in search of jobs abroad. These are no longer the manual workers of yesteryear who filled the factories of Germany, the mines of Belgium and the building sites of the UK. Now it is the young graduates who are on the move. In Portugal, the post-colonial flow has reversed, as hopefuls head out to Brazil, Angola and Mozambique in search of a better life. In Ireland, some churches have set up webcams so that émigré parishioners can watch services back home. Many have moved to other parts of Europe, notably Germany.

The story of how the European project was born, how the euro nearly died, how it was saved and how the EU should confront the dangers ahead is the subject of this book. The appendices provide a timeline, a glossary and the history of the crisis as told through covers of *The Economist*. Chapter 1 recounts the darkest days, when the European Central Bank (ECB), the International Monetary Fund (IMF) and others made secret preparations for the departure of Greece from the euro, and the possible collapse of the currency zone. The consequences, all agreed, were incalculable.

Chapter 2 shows how the idea of European integration was born from the political necessities of the early 1950s, with Europe emerging from the ruins of the second world war and then having to confront the challenge of the cold war. The euro was launched as a result of the failure of repeated attempts to fix exchange rates between European economies, and the desire to anchor a unified Germany more firmly within Europe after the collapse of the Berlin Wall.

The system that was created through successive treaties was a complex hybrid with elements of federalism and inter-governmentalism, a pantomime horse that was part United States and part United Nations. Chapter 3 explains the functioning of the EU, and the flawed structure of the euro, to help make clear how Europeans managed, and mismanaged, the crisis.

Chapter 4 shows how the launch of the euro was at first met with scepticism by outsiders, then treated with hubris by insiders. Blinkered by the fiscal rules, European institutions were for the most part unaware of the real danger to the monetary union. It did not come only, or mainly, from the accumulation of deficits and debt, which became easier for many countries to finance as interest rates fell. Rather, the bigger menace came from underlying external imbalances, with current-account deficits allowed to balloon in the belief that these would always be financed within a currency union.

As the financial crisis turned into a debt crisis in early 2010, European leaders and institutions muddled through from summit to summit, devising responses that were always too little, too late, and raised the cost for all. There were two broad phases, coinciding roughly with the tenures of Jean-Claude Trichet and Mario Draghi as presidents of the ECB, as noted in Chapters 5 and 6.

First there was a period of banking crises, bail-outs, austerity and debt restructuring – focused most acutely in Greece. This increasingly fraught time culminated in angry confrontations at the G20 summit in Cannes in November 2011, where the prime ministers of Greece and Italy were summoned for a dressing-down by fellow leaders and subsequently pushed out of office. In the second phase there was a growing realisation of the need to come up with a more systemic response. Seeking to halt the "doom-loop", in which weak banks and weak governments were dragging each other down, leaders embarked on the process of creating a banking union in June 2012. Soon thereafter, the ECB stepped in as a more credible lender of last resort for governments after Draghi declared the bank would do "whatever it takes" to stop the euro from breaking up.

The crisis has profoundly changed relations within the EU. It has confirmed Germany as the predominant power in Europe; it has shifted institutional power within Brussels from the European Commission to national governments; and it has caused a growing tension between euro ins and outs. This transformation is described in Chapters 7 and 8.

The crisis has also widened the democratic deficit in Europe, which the growing power of the European Parliament has been unable to fill, as explained in Chapter 9. Moreover, it has disrupted the core business of the EU that is often out of the headlines, from the single market to trade negotiations, as set out in Chapter 10, as well as the EU's hope of exerting greater influence on world affairs, a sorry tale recounted in Chapter 11.

The concluding Chapter 12 assesses the damage done by comparing the performance of the euro zone since the beginning of the global financial crisis with that of the United States. It tries to draw lessons from the upheaval and offers recommendations for reform. The main risks to the euro zone, and to the wider European Union, are now predominantly economic and political. The recovery is still weak, making it harder to bring down unacceptably high unemployment and leaving the euro zone vulnerable to a triple-dip recession, if not outright deflation. In turn, economic stagnation will worsen the growing polarisation of European politics.

The actions of European leaders may have averted collapse in the short term, but they have not found a lasting solution. The ECB's bond-buying policy stabilised debt markets but is untested, and Draghi's great bluff may not hold forever. The development of "economic governance", involving tougher fiscal rules and deeper intrusion by Brussels institutions into national economic policies, is unlikely to be accepted indefinitely. At some point, perhaps after the crisis has faded, national governments will want to reassert their autonomy. Discipline should be imposed by markets, not by Brussels. This means that governments should be allowed to go bust when they make a mess of their economic policies. In short, the no-bail-out rule needs to be restored. Doing so requires a euro zone stable enough to withstand the shock of a default. The answer, the conclusion argues, is a targeted dose of American-style fiscal federalism in which some of the risks are shared. This involves several reforms, from completing the embryonic banking union to issuing joint debt and perhaps setting up a modest central budget that can help stabilise economies. For the foreseeable future, the EU's crisis of legitimacy can be addressed only by enhancing the role of national parliaments.

None of this will be easy, but all of it will be necessary if the project of European integration is not just to survive but to thrive with the consent of its citizens.

John Peet and Anton La Guardia
March 2014

1   "If the euro fails, Europe fails"

IN THE SPRING AND SUMMER OF 2012 there was a fad in offering advice on how to break up the euro. More than two years after the start of the Greek debt crisis, the experiment of the single European currency seemed to be close to failure. Successive bail-outs, crushing austerity and innumerable emergency summits that produced at best a half-hearted response were stoking resentment among creditor and debtor countries alike. And since national leaders seemed either unwilling or unable to weld together a closer union, the pressure of the euro crisis was remorselessly pushing the cracks apart. Better, thought some, to attempt an orderly dissolution than to be confronted with a chaotic break-up.

In May the former chief economist at Deutsche Bank, Thomas Mayer, proposed the introduction of a parallel currency for Greece, a "Geuro", to help the country devalue.[1] In July Policy Exchange, a British think-tank, awarded the £250,000 Wolfson Prize for the best plan to break up the euro to Roger Bootle of Capital Economics,[2] a private research firm in London. The following month *The Economist* published a fictitious memorandum to Angela Merkel, the German chancellor, setting out two options for a break-up: the exit of Greece alone, and the departure of a larger group of five countries that added Cyprus, Spain, Portugal and Ireland as well. A footnote reported that the ever-cautious Merkel had turned down both possibilities, deeming the risks to be too great, and ordered the paper shredded. "No one need ever know that the German government had been willing to think the unthinkable. Unless, of course, the memo leaked."[3]

The imaginary memo was closer to the truth than readers might have thought. That summer Merkel did indeed ponder, and reject, the idea of throwing the Greeks out of the euro. German, European and IMF officials had by then drawn up detailed plans to manage a break-up of the euro – not to dissolve the currency completely but rather to try to preserve as much of it as possible if Greece (or another country) were to leave. The plans never leaked, which was just as well. The mere existence of a contingency plan for "Grexit" might have provoked a self-fulfilling panic in markets. Few had confidence that any plan to oversee an orderly break-up would work.

Officials thought the unthinkable on at least three occasions. The first was in November 2011, when Greece announced a referendum on its second bail-out programme. Germany and France, outraged by Greece's insubordination, demanded that the referendum question had to be whether Greece wanted to stay in the euro or not. For the first time, European leaders were openly entertaining the notion of Grexit. In the event the vote was abandoned after the fall, within days, of the prime minister, George Papandreou. The second moment of peril came between the two Greek elections in May and June of 2012, when the rise of radical parties of the left and the right increased the risk of the Greeks voting themselves out of the euro before cooler heads prevailed in the second ballot. (Even after the conservative leader, Antonis Samaras, had put together a government that belatedly committed itself to the EU adjustment programme, Merkel debated well into August over whether to expel Greece.) The third danger point was the tough negotiation over the bail-out for Cyprus in March 2013. The newly elected president, Nicos Anastasiades, threatened to leave the currency if a bail-out meant destroying the island's two largest banks and wiping out their big expatriate (mostly Russian) depositors. After two rounds of ugly negotiations Anastasiades succumbed to his rescuers.

The euro zone would have been ill-prepared to cope with Grexit in late 2011. Jean-Claude Trichet, who presided over the ECB until the end of October 2011, would not countenance detailed doomsday planning. And without the central bank's power to create money, a break-up might have been uncontrollable. Trichet's successor, Mario Draghi, did set up a crisis-management team in January 2012. Within a year the ECB and the IMF had developed an hour-by-hour, day-by-day plan to try to manage the departure of a euro-zone member.

By the time of the negotiations with Cyprus, admittedly a smaller country than Greece or the other rescued economies, the prospect of Cyprexit did not cause anywhere near the same degree of fear among officials, or markets.

Others also worked up contingency plans, not least in the European Commission and the European Council, though here co-ordination was weaker for fear of disclosure. "Everything in Brussels leaks," says one of those involved. Officials recount how on one occasion Herman Van Rompuy, president of the European Council, raised the prospect of Grexit with José Manuel Barroso, president of the Commission. "I don't want to know the details. But I hope you are taking care of it," Van Rompuy said. Even so, his own small team of economists also quietly worked up position papers.

It all made for a strange dance in the darkness. Within the Commission, staff at the economics directorate had been expressly ordered not to do any work on the response to a possible break-up, even though a discreet group of senior commissioners and officials did just that: plan for a split in the currency zone. They had two main purposes: first, to set out what would have to be done; and second, to make the case for why it should not be done. For others it was a matter of managing as well as possible. For all concerned a big dilemma was how much to tell the Greek authorities about the preparations for their country's possible return to the drachma. The answer was: hardly anything at all.

Like the gold standard, only worse

Fixed exchange-rate systems have fallen apart throughout history, from the gold standard to various dollar pegs. But giving up a fixed peg is very different from scrapping an entire currency. This has happened too, but usually only when political unions have broken apart: for instance, the break-up of the Austro-Hungarian empire, the collapse of the Soviet Union or the velvet divorce between the Czech Republic and Slovakia. And none of these precedents quite captures the special circumstances of the euro. It is a single currency without a single government. It is made up of rich countries, many of which have built up large debts and large external imbalances, so the sums at stake are proportionately large. A map of the world sized according to each country's government spending shows Europe as a huge, puffed-up ball of public money.[4] Moreover, the euro zone is a subset of the European Union and its single market, within which goods, services, capital and people move more or less freely. As a result, the spillover effects on other European countries would be that much greater.

It had taken years for countries to prepare for the introduction of the euro. If any left, they might have to adapt to the redenomination of a member's currency overnight, or at best over a weekend. Nobody could be sure about the consequences should the supposedly irrevocable currency become revocable. There were two prevailing beliefs. One was the amputation theory: severing a gangrenous limb such as Greece would save the rest of the body. The other was the domino theory: the fall of one country would lead to the collapse of one economy after another. Grexit might thus be followed by Portexit, Spexit, Italexit and even Frexit.

Given such uncertainties, the objective for officials preparing contingency plans was clear: regardless of which country left the euro, the rest must be held together almost at any cost. Those involved speak only in guarded terms about precisely what they would have done. Would the departure of, say, Greece have required Cyprus to leave as well, given their close interconnection? The ECB would have flooded the financial system with liquidity to try to ensure that credit markets did not dry up, as they had done after the collapse of Lehman Brothers, and to forestall runs on both banks and sovereigns. Large quantities of banknotes would have been made available in the south to reassure anxious depositors especially if, as during the Cyprus crisis, banks were shut down and capital controls imposed. The ECB would probably have engaged in unprecedented bond-buying to hold down the borrowing costs of vulnerable countries. Loans to countries already under bail-out programmes would have been increased, and some kind of precautionary loan extended to Spain and Italy.

The IMF would have helped Greece manage the reintroduction of the drachma. This would probably have required a transition period (perhaps as short as one month) involving a parallel currency, or

IOUs akin to the "patacones" that circulated in Argentina after it left its dollar peg in 2000, though EU lawyers thought these would be illegal. The ECB would have dealt with the technicalities of adapting European electronic payment systems to the departure of a member. The Commission would introduce guidelines for capital controls.

Greece might have needed additional aid to manage the upheaval, not least to buy essential goods. In what remained of the euro zone there would have been difficult decisions to take over the allocation of losses arising within the Eurosystem of central banks. National governments would have to decide who should be compensated for losses in case of default and the inevitable bankruptcies caused by the abrupt mismatch between assets and liabilities as the values of currencies shifted. They might also have increased deposit guarantees, although in some cases that might have done more harm than good if the additional liability endangered public finances in weaker countries – as it had done in Ireland in 2008.

Perhaps, thought some, there should be a Europe-wide deposit guarantee. Indeed, many thought there would have to be a dramatic political move towards greater integration. Nobody quite knew what form this might take, but it would have had to signal an unshakeable commitment to stay together. Without the infuriating Greeks, greater integration might even appear more feasible. Indeed, it was such a prospect that convinced some senior EU officials that it would be a good idea to let the Greeks go after all: not because contagion could be contained, as the Bundesbank would sometimes claim, but precisely because it could not. Grexit would be so awful that it would force governments to make a leap into federalism.

Safe, for now

All these considerations, and more, were on Merkel's mind in the summer of 2012 when she decided instead to keep the Greeks in. Beyond the financial price, Germany could not risk the political blame for breaking up the currency and, potentially, the European project itself. As she had repeatedly declared since the first bail-out of Greece in 2010, "if the euro fails, Europe fails".

Two other events changed the dynamics of the crisis. First, at a summit in June, Merkel and other leaders agreed to centralise financial supervision around the ECB and then have the option of recapitalising troubled banks directly from the euro zone's rescue funds. The move held out the promise, for the first time, of a banking union in which the risks of the financial sector would be shared. The aim was to break the doom-loop between weak banks and weak governments that threatened to destroy both, especially in Spain. The second, even more important, development that summer was Draghi's declared readiness to intervene in bond markets without pre-set limits, on condition that troubled countries sought a euro-zone bail-out and adjustment programme. He thus sharply raised the cost of betting against the euro – to the point that, at the time of writing in March 2014, Draghi's great bluff has yet to be called.

The euro has been saved, at least for a while. But even as economic output begins slowly to recover, the euro zone remains vulnerable and the wider European project remains under acute strain. As *The Economist*'s imaginary memo to Merkel noted, the contingency plans for the demise of the euro were never shredded; they were merely filed away. As *The Economist*'s imaginary memo to Merkel noted (see cover story headlined "Tempted, Angela?" in the issue of August 11th–17th in Appendix 4), the contingency plans for the demise of the euro were never shredded; they were merely filed away.

2 From the origins to Maastricht

THE EUROPEAN PROJECT was a consequence of the second world war and the cold war. How to tame the German problem that had led to two world wars? How to harness its economic power to rebuild Europe? And how to reconstitute the German army to help fend off the Soviet threat? The answer to these conundrums was to fuse the German economy within a common European system, and to embed its armed forces within a transatlantic military alliance.

Already in 1946, just a year after the war had ended, Churchill called in his Zurich speech for the creation of a "kind of United States of Europe", to be built on the basis of a partnership between France and Germany:[1]

> At present there is a breathing-space. The cannon have ceased firing. The fighting has stopped; but the dangers have not stopped. If we are to form the United States of Europe or whatever name or form it may take, we must begin now.

Four years later, with a strong nudge from the United States, the French foreign minister, Robert Schuman, produced a plan to integrate the coal and steel industries of France, Germany and anyone else who would want to join the project. This led directly to the creation of the European Coal and Steel Community (ECSC) in 1951.[2]

> The solidarity in production thus established will make it plain that any war between France and Germany becomes not merely unthinkable, but materially impossible. The setting up of this powerful productive unit, open to all countries willing to take part and bound ultimately to provide all the member countries with the

basic elements of industrial production on the same terms, will lay a true foundation for their economic unification.

This was the germ of the idea of European economic integration. Today the anniversary of the speech (May 9th) is celebrated as a holiday by the European institutions (known as Schuman Day). The ECSC encompassed not only France and Germany, but also Italy and the three Benelux countries, Belgium, the Netherlands and Luxembourg. Jean Monnet, a French civil servant and scion of a cognac-trading family, who was in many ways the *éminence grise* behind the entire European project, acted as the first president of its high authority.[3]

Schuman and Monnet followed the successful establishment of the ECSC with an attempt to set up a pan-European army, the European Defence Community. But this was a step too far for France. The plan was blocked by a vote in the French National Assembly in August 1954. Henceforth NATO would provide the necessary security umbrella, while European integration would focus on economic matters.

The Messina conference of 1955 prepared the ground for the signing in 1957 of the Treaty of Rome, under which the six European countries that had joined the ECSC established a European Economic Community (EEC), which proclaimed the objective of an "ever closer union". The treaty established a customs union and envisaged the progressive creation of a large unified economic area based on the "four freedoms" of movement – of people, services, goods and capital. The EEC is the direct forerunner of today's European Union.

Despite Churchill's ringing call in 1946, the UK, always a sceptic about European political integration, had stood aside from the process. Indeed, Churchill himself was clear that the UK would encourage but not join European integration. The British Labour government refused to sign up to Schuman's plan, with the then home secretary (and grandfather to a later European commissioner, Peter Mandelson), Herbert Morrison, declaring bluntly that "it's no good: the Durham miners won't wear it".[4] A later Tory government sent only a junior official to Messina, with clear instructions not to sign up to anything. Yet by 1961, only four years after the Treaty of Rome, the Macmillan government lodged an application for membership, only to see it blocked by Charles de Gaulle's veto in January 1963.

Currency roots

The notion of a single currency was present at the very creation of the European project. Jacques Rueff, a French economist, wrote in the 1950s that "Europe will be made through the currency, or it will not be made".[5] The idea of a common currency has even earlier roots. Various exchange-rate regimes emerged in 19th-century Europe, including the Zollverein (customs union) and the gold standard. The Latin Monetary Union, set up in 1866, embraced a particularly unlikely sounding group: France, Italy, Belgium, Switzerland, Spain, Greece, Romania and Bulgaria (even more bizarrely, Venezuela later joined it). When it started Walter Bagehot, editor of *The Economist*, delivered a warning that has a curious echo today:[6]

> *If we do nothing, what then? Why, we shall be left out in the cold ... Before long, all Europe, save England, will have one money, and England be left standing with another money.*

In the event, the Latin Monetary Union fell apart when it was hit by the disaster of the first world war.

The 1930s was another period of currency instability in Europe – and the world. The UK and the Scandinavian countries all chose to do the unthinkable in 1931 by leaving the gold standard and devaluing. A rival "gold block" led by France and including Italy, the Netherlands and Switzerland, chose to stay on the gold standard until 1935–36. As Nicholas Crafts showed in a 2013 paper for Chatham House, the early leavers did much better in terms of GDP and employment than the stayers – and France, which suffered a lot from clinging so long to gold, played a role equivalent to today's Germany by hoarding the stuff and also insisting on running large current-account surpluses.[7]

Although the desire for currency stability carried through into the early years of the European project, the global system of fixed exchange rates linked to the dollar (and thus to gold) set up after the 1944 Bretton Woods conference that established the International Monetary Fund (IMF) and the World Bank seemed sufficient for most countries. But over time, and especially in France, the perception was growing that this system gave the Americans some sort of exorbitant privilege. This was one reason why the European Commission first formally proposed a single European currency in 1962. By the end of the decade, the revaluation of Germany's Deutschmark against the French franc in 1969 created fresh trauma in both countries, which turned into renewed worries when the United States formally abandoned its link to gold two years later.

As the difficulty of living with a dominant but devaluing dollar increased, Willy Brandt, then German chancellor, revived plans for a currency union in Europe. His plan was taken up in the 1971 Werner report, named after a Luxembourgish prime minister, which argued for the adoption of a single currency by 1980. The report was endorsed in 1972 by all European heads of government, including those from the three countries that planned to join the club in 1973: Denmark, Ireland and the UK. Indeed, at a summit meeting of heads of government in Paris in December 1972, all nine national leaders, including the UK's Edward Heath, signed up blithely not only to monetary union but also to political union by 1980. A last-minute attempt by the Danish prime minister to ask his colleagues exactly what was meant by political union was ignored by the French president, Georges Pompidou, who was in the chair.[8]

It was the final collapse of Bretton Woods, followed by the Arab-Israeli war and oil shock and then by the global recession of 1974–75, that upset most of these ambitious plans. Yet by then West Germany, always on the look-out for greater currency stability, had already set up a system linking most of Europe's currencies to the Deutschmark, swiftly dubbed the "snake in the tunnel". The idea was to set limits to bilateral currency fluctuations, enforced by central-bank intervention. However, it turned out that the snake had only a fitful and unsatisfactory life. The UK signed up in mid-1972, only to be forced out by the financial markets six weeks later. Both France and Italy joined and left the snake twice. Devaluations within the system were distressingly frequent.

By 1978 there was still no sign of a general return to the Bretton

Woods system of fixed exchange rates. So Europe's political leaders came up with the idea of creating a grander version of the snake in the form of a European Monetary System (EMS). The EMS was mainly the brainchild of the French president, Valéry Giscard d'Estaing, and the German chancellor, Helmut Schmidt, although the president of the European Commission, Roy Jenkins, acted as midwife. In March 1979, the EMS came into being. Its main provision was an exchange-rate mechanism that limited European currency fluctuations to 2¼% either side of a central rate (or to 6% for those with wider bands). All nine members of the European Community joined the system – except, as so often, the UK (this meant, incidentally, that the EMS broke up one of Europe's few existing monetary unions, that between the UK and Ireland).

Yet for all its ambitions, the EMS proved only a little more permanent and solid than the snake. Italy was at best a fitful and wobbly member. And the election in 1981 of François Mitterrand as France's first Socialist president of the Fifth Republic led to repeated devaluations of the franc – until the president, under the guidance of his new finance minister, Jacques Delors, and his most senior treasury official, Jean-Claude Trichet, adopted a new policy of *le franc fort*. When a year or two later Delors arrived in Brussels as the new president of the European Commission, he was quick once again to dust down the old plans for a European single currency.

Enter Delors

The result was the Delors report, commissioned by European leaders in June 1988, which advocated a three-stage move towards European economic and monetary union (EMU). First, complete the single market, including the free movement of capital. Second, prepare for the creation of the European Central Bank and ensure economic convergence. Third, fix exchange rates and launch the euro, first as a currency of reckoning and then as notes and coins. The Delors report went on to form the basis of the Maastricht treaty, negotiated over 18 months and finally agreed on, with much fanfare, in the eponymous Dutch city in December 1991. The treaty was formally signed only in February 1992. Maastricht laid the foundations for a new ECB and a single European currency, to be brought in either in 1997 or (at the latest) 1999. It also promised to make progress towards the parallel objective of political union; and it symbolically renamed the European Community the European Union.

The new treaty reflected above all the changed political situation in Europe after the fall of the Berlin Wall in November 1989 and the subsequent collapse of the Soviet empire. Mitterrand, in particular, was minded to accept German unification after the fall of the wall only if France could secure some control of the Deutschmark, which he feared would otherwise become Europe's de facto currency. In effect, he had no wish to replace the dominance of the dollar with the dominance of the Deutschmark. Hence the underlying Franco-German deal at Maastricht.

The French had long favoured a new single currency, over which they hoped (vainly, as it turned out) to exert greater influence, in large part to offset the growing might of a newly powerful united Germany. In his turn, the German chancellor, Helmut Kohl, accepted the idea of giving up the Deutschmark, which many German voters as well as the Bundesbank were against, as a price for unification and as a giant step towards building a political union in Europe. Other countries signed up to this with more or less enthusiasm. As usual, the British concern was mainly to be allowed to opt out if they wanted, an objective that was easily secured by John Major, the prime minister, who told the press that the result was "game, set and match" to the UK.[9]

Besides a general (especially German) desire for currency stability and a wish to contain the power of a united Germany, two other forces were important in driving Europe along the road towards Maastricht and the decision to adopt a single currency. One was theoretical: the literature on shared currencies that began with Robert Mundell's 1961 article outlining a theory of "optimum currency areas". Mundell, a Canadian economics professor, posited that substantial welfare gains were to be had if a group of countries shared a currency – because of more transparent prices, lower transaction costs, enhanced competition and greater economies of scale for businesses and investors. But these gains needed to be weighed against the possible costs from losing both monetary and exchange-rate independence.[10]

Such costs, according to optimal currency-area theory, risked being especially high if the countries concerned suffered from internal labour- or product-market rigidities, had very different economic structures or were likely to be subject to asymmetric shocks. The theory went on to look at how groups of countries that did not meet these conditions could be changed to make them more suitable. The obvious remedies were more flexibility, notably in labour and product markets; greater labour mobility, so that workers who lost jobs in one country could move freely to countries with more job opportunities; and a substantial central budget that could transfer resources to countries that got into trouble. The 1977 MacDougall report had argued that, in the early stages of a European federal union, a central budget would have to be at least 5–7% of Europe-wide GDP, excluding defence (that is, 5–7 times the size of the existing European budget), if it was to be effective.[11]

The second force driving monetary union was a more practical one: the move towards a full single market that was being pushed forward by the Delors Commission, most notably by the British commissioner of the time, Arthur Cockfield. The Single European Act, approved and ratified in 1986–87, had paved the way for much greater use of qualified-majority voting (that is, a system of weighted majority as opposed to unanimity) on most directives and regulations. This was crucial to the adoption of the 1992 programme for completing the single market. With this step, what was about to become the European Union at last embraced, more or less in full, the four freedoms that had supposedly underpinned the project from its very beginnings: free movement of goods, services, labour and capital (the last remaining capital controls were abolished in 1990).[12]

The link between the single market and the single currency is not always clear, especially to Eurosceptics, who tend to prefer the first to the second. The reason it exists lies mostly in the fourth of the four freedoms: movement of capital. It is best summed up by the notion of the "impossible trinity" that became popular in the economics literature in the 1980s: the combination of free movement of capital, wholly national monetary policies and independent control of exchange rates was declared to be unworkable or even impossible because the three were likely to contradict each other. The solution, it was held both in the literature and by Europe's political leaders, was not to revert to constraints on capital flows, still less to unpick the single market, but instead to press forward to a single currency.

Yet Mundell's work also showed quite clearly that, outside a limited central group, Europe was a long way from being an optimal currency area. Labour and product markets were inflexible and overregulated. Workers' mobility was limited, not just for obvious linguistic and cultural reasons between countries but even within them. Asymmetric shocks, far from being rare, were worryingly common: German unification was itself an example of one, as was the collapse of Finland's trade with Russia in 1990 and the bursting of various property bubbles in the 1980s. And countries' economies varied widely: Germany was strong in manufacturing but weak in services, whereas the UK was the reverse, for example, while national housing and mortgage markets differed hugely in their structure, operation, importance and sensitivity to interest-rate changes. The Maastricht negotiators were well aware of such problems, although many were swift to point out that the United States had a single currency without really being an optimal currency area either. But there were crucial differences between the American system and the euro zone.

Perhaps ironically, it was the UK's David Cameron, prime minister of a country that will probably never join the single currency, who best summed up these defects, speaking 12 years after the euro was launched at a Davos World Economic Forum. As he then put it:[13]

> There are a number of features common to all successful currency unions: a central bank that can comprehensively stand behind the currency and financial system; the deepest possible economic integration with the flexibility to deal with economic shocks; and a system of fiscal transfers and collective debt issuance that can deal with the tensions and imbalances between different countries and regions within the union. Currently it's not that the euro zone doesn't have all of these; it's that it doesn't really have any of these.

Instead of creating such structures, the creators of the euro limited themselves to devising a set of "convergence criteria" that national governments would be required to meet in order to qualify for membership of the European single currency. Yet, as many argued even at the time, they quite irresponsibly chose ones that had little to do with transforming Europe into something that might have more closely resembled an optimal currency area.

The right debate at Maastricht would have been about how best to push forward structural reforms to labour and product markets, how to improve countries' competitiveness and current-account positions, how to create a backstop system of transfers or insurance and how to make sure that the putative European Central Bank could act properly as a lender of last resort. Plenty of commentators, including many from the United States and the UK, made such observations. One example was an article in *The Economist* in October 1998, which concluded:[14]

> *The current set-up looks unsatisfactory. The ECB should be recognised as lender of last resort. It could also be given central responsibility for financial-sector supervision.*

In the event, the five criteria chosen for the Maastricht treaty were: low inflation and low long-term interest rates; two years' membership of the exchange-rate mechanism of the EMS; and, most controversially of all, ceilings on public debt of 60% of GDP and on budget deficits of 3% of GDP. Why were these last two tests chosen? The leaders of more prudent countries (that is, Germany and the Netherlands) argued that, if the single currency were to pass muster with sceptical financial markets and public opinion, limits would have to be set on potentially profligate public borrowers (by which they chiefly meant Italy and the Mediterranean countries).

But the truth was a lot more political. German voters were still hostile to the idea of giving up the Deutschmark. One reason was a widespread fear that Germany might end up having to bail out Europe's most indebted countries, especially the most indebted of all: Italy. Thus the debt and deficit criteria were devised not so much on their economic merits, but rather in the expectation that they would keep Italy (and presumably also Spain, Portugal and Greece) out of the single currency, as these countries were expected to find it all but impossible to pass the two fiscal tests. The hope, in short, was that

EMU would begin smoothly but with a small core group, essentially the Deutschmark zone plus (almost certainly) France.

Ready, steady, go

Two big events overturned this tidy plan. The first, which coincided ominously with the negotiation and signature of the Maastricht treaty, was yet another bout of financial-market jitters. Throughout the trauma of German unification, the EMS and its exchange-rate mechanism had continued to operate. Indeed, the UK chose to join in mid-1990, after a long and politically controversial experiment by the then chancellor of the exchequer, Nigel Lawson, to "shadow" the Deutschmark without informing his prime minister, Margaret Thatcher. The strain of keeping up with a strong Deutschmark soon began to tell, and it was considerably increased in November 1990 by the ousting of Thatcher, largely over the issue of the UK's attitude to plans for the new European treaty that later became Maastricht.

But it was the aftermath of German unification in that same month that really got the markets going. This asymmetric shock may have cost West Germany a lot of treasure and required massive new investment, but its effect in the marketplace was to increase demand for the German currency. That sent the Deutschmark soaring, hitting German competitiveness at a time when much of Europe was on the verge of recession or actually in it. The markets became even more jittery when, in a June 1992 referendum, the Danes narrowly said no to the recently signed Maastricht treaty. In early September French voters said yes, but by the thinnest possible majority. By then the strains on the UK, Italy and France itself of supporting their exchange rates to keep up with the Deutschmark had grown intolerable. In a dramatic week in mid-September, first Italy and then the UK were forced out of the EMS's exchange-rate mechanism. And the German Bundesbank had to intervene heavily to keep France in (a trick it repeated in late 1993, when the permissible bands in the exchange-rate mechanism were widened to 15%).

Those involved in what the British later came to call "Black Wednesday" drew very different conclusions from it. France became convinced that a single currency, over which it still hoped to exert some political control, was more essential than ever, for without it the Bundesbank would remain paramount. The UK concluded that a currency straitjacket was a bad idea and that it could never rely on German support, so Black Wednesday came to be seen as another reason to stay out of a single currency, if one ever came into being (it is worth recalling that a young Cameron was a political adviser to the chancellor of the exchequer, Norman Lamont, at the time of Black Wednesday). Italy, Spain and other Mediterranean countries drew a different lesson still: they decided that, while a single currency might well impose pain on them, it would be better to do whatever they could to hop on board from the beginning rather than risk falling further behind.

Hence also the second big development in the 1990s: the response of the Mediterranean countries, most of which the Germans still wanted to keep out. The test case was Italy. In the early 1990s its budget deficit and, even more obviously, its public debt were way above the Maastricht targets. Yet there was bound to be some flexibility in the system, not least because Belgium, which as the seat of the European institutions and part of the Benelux trio was seen by all as an essential founder member of EMU, also had a public debt in excess of 100% of GDP. In 1996 Romano Prodi, who had become Italian prime minister just over a year earlier, spoke to his Spanish counterpart, José Maria Aznar, about the possibility of jointly standing aside from the third stage of EMU when it came. But Aznar replied that he, at least, was determined to join from the start. That drove Prodi not only to rejoin the EMS but also to redouble his efforts to cut Italy's budget deficit to below 3% of GDP. Given the Belgian position, it was always going to be hard to exclude Italy on the grounds of its public debt alone. This became truer still when France and to some extent Germany itself had to massage their budget numbers to get below the 3% ceiling in 1997 and 1998.

As the likelihood that Italy would be a founder member of the single currency became ever more obvious, the German finance minister, Theo Waigel, started to press harder for a formalisation and tightening of the rules limiting budget deficits and debts after EMU had started, as well as before. The Maastricht treaty had laid down an excessive deficits procedure, but Waigel felt that it was too flexible.

Instead, he demanded a new "stability pact" that would automatically impose swingeing fines on any country that ran a budget deficit above 3% of GDP. Most other countries, led by France, naturally resisted any automatic sanctions.

Eventually Waigel was forced to give ground: the fines would be imposed only with the approval of a "qualified majority" of member governments (excluding the miscreant). When in France a new Socialist government was formed after the party won the parliamentary election of June 1997, he even had to concede a change of name to turn it into a "stability and growth pact". Ironically enough, his own boss, Helmut Kohl, lost his job just over a year later to his Social Democratic challenger. This meant that the two original champions of the euro – Kohl and Mitterrand – had both left office by the time it actually began (and the two countries also had nominally centre-left governments in 1999). Their successors as German and French leaders, Gerhard Schröder and Jacques Chirac, felt less committed either to the euro in general or to the stability and growth pact in particular. Indeed, they were to become the first to breach its terms, in late 2003.

By late 1997, then, it was clear that all EU countries except Denmark, Sweden and the UK, all of which had opted out in one way or another, and Greece, which was miles from meeting any of the criteria, would join the euro when it began life in 1999. Physical notes and coins followed only in 2002, partly because of the time said to be needed to print and mint them in sufficient quantities. In the meantime Greece quietly slipped in to join the single currency at the start of 2001, at a time when few people were looking. Perhaps worryingly, this echoed the story of Greece's entry into the EEC in 1981. The Commission had given a negative opinion on Greece's application, but it was overruled by national governments largely on the basis that, as France's classically minded president, Valéry Giscard d'Estaing, put it, "one does not say no to Plato".[15] It also helped that Greece's prime minister in 2001, Costas Simitis, was both Germanophile and German-speaking. After Greece joined, the fun really began.

3   How it all works

THE EUROPEAN PROJECT (and thus the euro) suffers both from a lack of clarity over its precise nature and end-point and from the dull complexity of its institutional structure. Like a pantomime horse, it has long had a dual character, reflecting an initial compromise between those countries wanting a United States of Europe and those preferring a club of nation-states. Thus it has federalist elements such as the European Commission, a (now directly elected) European Parliament, a European Court of Justice and a European Central Bank. But it also has strong inter-governmental bodies: the Council of Ministers, representing national governments, and the European Council of heads of state and government. An important force throughout the euro crisis has been the tension between those preferring federal answers (often called the "community" method) and those favouring inter-governmental solutions (sometimes referred to as the "union" method).[1]

At the heart of both the EU and the euro stands the European Commission, to which each of the currently 28 national governments appoints one commissioner for a five-year term (the next Commission takes office at the end of 2014). Commissioners, based in Brussels, are legally required to be wholly independent, although in practice they usually do what they can to advance national interests. The "college" of 28 commissioners sits above a 20,000-strong bureaucracy that functions as the European Union's executive branch. The Commission is the guardian of the treaties, has the near-exclusive right of legislative initiative, administers competition and state-aid law and conducts certain third-party negotiations, for instance on trade, on behalf of the EU as a whole.

The Council of Ministers is the senior legislative body. It consists of ministers from national governments, meeting in different formations (finance or EcoFin, agriculture and fisheries, environment, and so on). In many areas the Council takes decisions by qualified majority, a system of weighted votes that, under the 2009 Lisbon treaty, is due to change in late 2014 into a new arrangement of a "double majority" that takes greater account of population size. Council meetings are prepared by officials in the Committee of Permanent Representatives in Brussels (COREPER); EcoFin meetings are often prepared by the official-level Economic and Financial Committee; and there is also a euro working group. The Council presidency rotates every six months from one country to another, though this system has been modified, under Lisbon, by the arrival of a permanent president of the European Council and a high representative for foreign policy, who chairs Council meetings of foreign ministers as well as being a vice-president of the Commission.

The European Council is, in effect, the most senior formation of the Council of Ministers. It did not exist at the start of the European project, but over time the practice of calling occasional summit meetings of heads of state and government to give general direction and to resolve the most contentious disputes became habitual. Under Lisbon, the European Council has a full-time president, currently Belgium's Herman Van Rompuy, who serves for a maximum of five years (his term expires at the end of 2014). Van Rompuy has set the pattern of holding European Council meetings every two months or so. These summits have often received much publicity, especially during the euro crisis when they have often drifted into weekends and the early hours of the morning. Over time, the European Council has become the strategic engine of the European Union, largely displacing the Commission, a switch that has become even clearer as a result of the euro crisis.

The Commission makes most of its legislative proposals jointly to the Council and the European Parliament, the second legislative body in the EU. The Parliament, which has been directly elected since 1979, now has 751 members. At French insistence, it is formally based in Strasbourg for most of its monthly plenary sessions, although its committees and most of its members (MEPs) are generally based in Brussels. Elections are held every five years: the 2014 ones are scheduled to take place between May 22nd and May 25th. Successive treaties have given the Parliament ever-greater powers, and it is now more or less co-equal with the Council of Ministers in legislation. The European Parliament must approve the annual budget as well as the multi-annual financial framework. It can reject the budget (it did so in December 1979). Unlike the Council, it can also sack the Commission (it used this power to force the Santer Commission's resignation in 1999). And, again under Lisbon, the Parliament now has the power to "elect" the Commission president, after he or she is nominated by the European Council, a provision that creates an obvious risk of a huge institutional bust-up.

The most important remaining institution is the European Court of Justice, based in Luxembourg, which acts as the European Union's supreme court and adjudicates on disputes both among the institutions and between countries in areas of EU competence (so it has no role in the criminal law, for example). The court has one judge per country, though there is also a Court of First Instance to reduce its workload. Cases are usually decided by simple majority. The Court of Justice (not to be confused with the Strasbourg-based European Court of Human Rights, part of the Council of Europe) has advanced European integration in several judgments, notably the 1963 *Van Gend en Loos* case, which established the principle of the supremacy of European over national law, and the 1979 *Cassis de Dijon* judgment, which laid down that goods sold in one country must be able to be sold in all. Other EU bodies include the Court of Auditors and the European Investment Bank, both based in Luxembourg, the Economic and Social Committee and the Committee of Regions, both based in Brussels – and a plethora of smaller agencies scattered right across Europe.[2]

These institutions operate collectively by the "community method". This describes the classical path of EU legislation: a proposal is made by the Commission; it is adopted by co-decision between the Council and the European Parliament, often followed by "trilogue" between the two and the Commission to reconcile their positions; it is then implemented by national authorities and is subject to the jurisdiction of the Court of Justice. But at many times in the past, and again during the euro crisis, national governments, especially those of the UK and France, have jibbed against the community method. President de Gaulle's Fouchet plan would have set up inter-governmental institutions alongside the Brussels machinery. The Maastricht treaty introduced two new "pillars" for foreign and security policy and for justice and home affairs, in which the roles of the Commission and the Parliament were limited and legislation was not generally justiciable at the Court of Justice, unlike most other EU activities.

In practice most such efforts to work outside the "community method" have proved unsatisfactory. The Fouchet plan did not get anywhere. The Maastricht pillars have, under the Lisbon treaty, been subsumed back within the first pillar. Yet many national governments, including now Germany, still like the simplicity of working inter-governmentally. During the euro crisis, Angela Merkel has often praised the "union method", which downgrades the roles of the Commission, the Parliament and the Court of Justice.

Enter the ECB

Several institutions for the single currency were bolted onto the system after the Maastricht treaty was ratified. Foremost among these is the European Central Bank, which started work in June 1998 (it had a forerunner, the European Monetary Institute, set up in 1994). The ECB, which at German insistence is based in Frankfurt, home of the Bundesbank, sits at the apex of what is called the European System of Central Banks, to which all national central banks belong (even those from EU countries still outside the euro). The ECB has a six-strong executive board, headed by a president and a vice-president, all of whom serve single eight-year terms. Its governing council consists of this board plus the governors of the national central banks of countries in the euro. It normally takes decisions by simple majority. The initial system of one vote per council member is to be superseded, most probably during 2015, by an arrangement that will give the executive board six votes, add four votes that rotate among the five biggest euro members and give the rest, no matter how many there are, 11 votes in total (this change creates at least the theoretical possibility that the Bundesbank's president might not always have a vote on the council).

The ECB was modelled on the German Bundesbank but is in many ways even more powerful and independent. Its goal, fixed by the Maastricht treaty, is price stability (close to but below 2%), whereas the Federal Reserve, its American counterpart, is also required to pay attention to employment. Its operational independence in delivering the goal of price stability, which it defines itself, is also guaranteed by the same treaty. Unlike other central banks, it has no single government or finance ministry to interact with and report to, though its president testifies before the European Parliament and attends most meetings of the European Council and often EcoFin and the Eurogroup as well. In line with the Bundesbank model, when EMU arrived the ECB was not given overall responsibility for bank supervision, which stayed at national level, an arrangement that has since been deemed unsatisfactory, with the planned "banking union" giving supervision of most large European banks to the ECB. It also had no obligation to act as the system's lender of last resort, a huge potential problem once it took over the operation of monetary policy from national central banks.

One big difference between the ECB and most other central banks is that it is much smaller (it has a staff of less than 1,000) and also, because of the continuing role of the national central banks, a lot more decentralised. That makes the role of the president, the ECB's public face, especially important. Given this, it was foolish and dangerous when the European Council chose to welcome the new bank with an all-day wrangle in May 1998 over who should be its president. The job had long been intended to go to Wim Duisenberg, a former Dutch central banker who had run the European Monetary Institute. But at the last minute the French president, Jacques Chirac, put forward Jean-Claude Trichet for the job. The outcome was a botched and undignified compromise in which the term was informally split between the two men. Duisenberg stepped down in 2003, leaving Trichet to serve a complete eight-year term, until he in turn was replaced by an Italian, Mario Draghi, in 2011.

The lack of any strong political authority to act as a counterpart to the ECB was obvious from the start. The Commission has scarcely more accountability than the bank. The European Parliament is elected, but it has no executive authority. The European Council and EcoFin include non-members of the euro. From an early stage the French pushed for the creation of some form of "economic government", but the Germans resisted the concept in order to safeguard the ECB's independence. Instead, in 1998 European governments came up with the idea of a "Eurogroup" of finance ministers. Finance ministers from non-euro countries fiercely resisted the Eurogroup's establishment. The UK's Gordon Brown, then chancellor of the exchequer, tried hard to join as an observer at the group's first meeting at the Château de Senningen in Luxembourg in June 1997, only to be told by his French counterpart, Dominique Strauss-Kahn, that the euro was like a marriage and that, in a marriage, one did not invite strangers into the bedroom (a precept that Strauss-Kahn has followed only erratically in his own life).

In any event the Eurogroup soon became accepted, and it even acquired its own permanent chairman: first, Jean-Claude Juncker, Luxembourg's prime minister and finance minister, and then, from the end of 2012, Jeroen Dijsselbloem, the Dutch finance minister. By this time it had also become accepted, once again over objections from countries outside the euro, supported by Germany, that European heads of government should meet periodically in euro-zone summits, usually just after full European Councils. In either formation, the Eurogroup has no statutory basis and no legislative powers. But it has become an essential part of the single currency's architecture.

Another component is the "excessive deficit procedure". This began in the Maastricht treaty and was reformulated into the stability and growth pact, which was approved in 1997. However, from the very beginning the rules against excessive deficits and public-debt levels were interpreted flexibly, not least so that Belgium and Italy could join the single currency. The stability pact's provisions for sanctions were watered down in negotiation from being automatic, as the Germans originally wanted, to requiring qualified-majority approval by the Council. Even so, the pact attracted much criticism from economists, who felt that, given euro-zone countries' loss of an independent monetary and exchange-rate policy, more not less fiscal flexibility might be needed. It was also thought that imposing central rules might undermine the force of the treaty's "no-bail-out" provisions, because it would imply a high degree of central intrusion. Better, many argued, to rely on the bond markets to impose discipline on any country that borrowed so much that it looked to be at risk of defaulting.[3]

The pact's credibility was further dented in 2002 when Romano Prodi, president of the Commission, called it "stupid". Portugal was the first country to get into difficulties, and it was duly required to amend its budget to comply with the pact. But it was never likely to constrain bigger countries and, in late 2003, its potency was almost entirely destroyed when France and, ironically, Germany itself persuaded the Council to override a Commission recommendation that both countries should cut their budget deficits, which had drifted above 3% of GDP.[4]

The gutting of the stability pact made it less of a surprise, when the financial crisis hit in 2008, that the deficits and debt levels of most euro-zone countries went above the Maastricht ceilings. Naturally, the crisis also prompted calls for a revival of the excessive deficits procedure, but with new teeth. Its new incarnation, adopted in late 2011, includes the "two-pack" and "six-pack" and sets out a "European semester". Euro-zone countries now have to submit their draft budgets to the Commission in advance, and the Commission can request changes before national parliaments even have a chance to consider them. A new excessive imbalances procedure has also been added, enabling the Commission to monitor and make recommendations for countries that, among other things, run large current-account imbalances (defined, with a nod to chronically underconsuming Germany, as 4% of GDP for deficits but 6% of GDP for surpluses).

In terms of sanctions, the new procedures look similar to the old except that now a Commission recommendation will be automatically adopted unless a qualified majority in the Council votes against it. Such a negative qualified-majority procedure is also enshrined in the "fiscal compact" treaty, which was approved and ratified in 2012 as an inter-governmental treaty using the "union method", partly because several governments including France's and Germany's liked it that way, partly because the UK and the Czech Republic refused to sign it (the Czechs now plan to do so) and partly because it allowed the treaty's drafters to provide that it would come into force even if some countries failed to ratify it. The fiscal compact requires all signatories to insert debt brakes into their national constitutional arrangements.

It also formalises, with the Euro Plus Pact, the existence of euro summits, alongside European Councils.

The euro crisis has added a set of further, ad hoc pieces to the single currency's institutional architecture, many of them also set up on the union method. First came the temporary European Financial Stability Facility (EFSF), an inter-governmental vehicle set up in a rush after the rescue of Greece in May 2010. Alongside this there is a smaller European Financial Stability Mechanism, which uses the EU budget as collateral. Both funds are being subsumed into the permanent treaty-based European Stability Mechanism (ESM). The ESM was set up as an organisation under public international law with a board of governors (that is, finance ministers) and a managing director, Klaus Regling, previously the Commission's economics director-general. Although an inter-governmental body, the ESM has operational links to the Commission and is also subject to the jurisdiction of the European Court of Justice.

Treaties, treaties

One reason it is often hard for outsiders to understand how either the EU or the euro works is that, for the past 25 years or so, the entire European project has been going through a veritable orgy of treaty-making. After the Single European Act of 1986 and the Maastricht treaty, signed in February 1992, there was but a short pause before the Amsterdam treaty of 1997 and then the Nice treaty of 2001. Each time, it seemed, the driving force for successive treaties was a widespread feeling of dissatisfaction at what had been done on the previous occasion and at what had failed to be agreed or had been left out. The expansion of the European Union to take in Austria, Finland and Sweden in 1995 and, in a far bigger challenge, eight central and eastern European countries from the former Soviet block plus Cyprus and Malta in 2004 was another consideration.

Even as the euro emerged from infancy in December 2001, just before the date for the issue of euro notes and coins, EU leaders, meeting in Laeken in Belgium, decided to have one more go at their governing treaties. This time they set up a convention on the future of Europe, chaired by a former French president, Valéry Giscard d'Estaing, which swiftly decided, amid much excited chatter drawing analogies with Philadelphia in 1787, to draw up a complete new constitution for the EU. The text of this constitutional treaty was broadly endorsed by an inter-governmental conference and then adopted at a European Council meeting in 2004. But after that the trouble began, because no fewer than ten countries announced plans to put the draft constitution to national referendums before ratification.[5]

Several treaty referendums had been held before, and in some cases treaties had been rejected only to be put to the vote again (this happened in Denmark over Maastricht and Ireland over Nice). But never had so many referendums been promised at once. In the event, it should not have come as a huge surprise when two of the first four said no: in France on May 29th 2005 and then in the Netherlands on June 3rd 2005, in both cases by large majorities. The expedient of making a few modifications and asking single small countries to vote again was clearly not going to work with such large founder members. So the constitution was abandoned.

The immediate impact of this setback on the euro may have seemed slight. But it fostered a broader sense of crisis in the EU as a whole. One reason was that it made everybody leery of further attempts at treaty change, a feeling that has persisted into the euro crisis. The gloom was intensified by the coincidence of yet another row over the EU's budget. Although the budget is small, at little more than 1% of EU-wide GDP, its excessive spending on agriculture and its skewed net benefits have caused repeated arguments at least since Margaret Thatcher came to power in the UK in 1979 and promptly demanded "my money back". Her determined handbagging of fellow European leaders eventually produced a series of ad hoc rebates, followed by a permanent abatement of the net British budget contribution, which was agreed at a European Council in Fontainebleau in 1984.[6]

Despite this deal, subsequent negotiations on the EU's multi-annual financial framework have proved almost equally contentious, and the one in 2005 was no exception. The UK, which wanted a smaller budget, less spending on agriculture and to preserve its rebate untouched, was once again in the doghouse, but several other countries favoured budgetary cuts while the new members from central and eastern Europe wanted far more spending. A compromise was reached only at the end of the year, when the British prime minister, Tony Blair, gave up part of the rebate to ensure that the UK would bear a fair share of the costs of enlargement to the east. But the sour atmosphere helped to cloud much other business, including that of the euro. Juncker, as president of the Council, declared that the EU was "in deep crisis".

The gloom also spilt over into the other big issue facing European leaders at the start of 2006: what to do about the failed constitutional treaty. On this the key person was the new German chancellor, Angela Merkel, who took office in late 2005 at the head of a "grand coalition" between her Christian Democrats and the Social Democrats. She was determined to revive as much as she could from the constitution, not least because the new voting system that it proposed at long last recognised that Germany's population is larger than that of other EU countries. After her fellow centre-right leader, Nicolas Sarkozy, became French president in mid-2007, the two pressed ahead with what later became the Lisbon treaty, which incorporated most of what had been in the constitution but in a disguised and less comprehensible fashion.

Critics complained that reviving the treaty in this way was a backdoor route around the negative votes in France and the Netherlands. They objected even more vociferously when almost all EU leaders, including the French and the Dutch, said they would not try to ratify Lisbon by referendums but use parliamentary votes instead. The exception was Ireland, which was constitutionally required to hold a referendum. Yet again, Irish voters said no, this time in June 2008. But just over a year later, after the financial crisis had struck, they were persuaded to change their minds in a fresh vote, so Lisbon was finally approved in late 2009. The new permanent president of the European Council, Herman Van Rompuy of Belgium, and the new high representative for foreign and security policy, Baroness Catherine Ashton of the UK, were chosen at a summit shortly afterwards, after yet another wrangle. But by then the focus of attention was starting to shift to the crisis in Greece – and particularly to the fiscal problems of a newly elected Greek Socialist government.

4 Build-up to a crisis

IF THERE IS AN ORIGINAL SIN in the creation of the euro, it is, for many in Berlin and Brussels, the breach of the stability and growth pact in 2003. Germany and France colluded to block any official rebuke or sanctions for letting their budget deficits rise above the Maastricht ceiling of 3% of GDP. After a battle with the European Commission that ended up at the European Court of Justice, they negotiated a looser version of the pact in 2005 that, to critics, rendered it toothless. From then on, so the story goes, all semblance of fiscal discipline was abandoned. Today's German ministers castigate their predecessors for leading the euro zone into sin rather than virtue. Yet this account offers at best only a partial explanation of what went wrong.

It is true that countries that tightened their belts to qualify for membership of the single currency relaxed their reforming effort after it started life in 1999. Many felt that it was enough to have proved wrong the doom-mongers in the UK and the United States who had predicted either that the euro would never arrive or that it would quickly break up (at one point in 1999, when it fell in value, it was christened a "toilet currency" by traders in London; others referred to the euro as the "zero"). Moreover, as Europe then entered a mild recession in 2001–02 there were others, beyond France and Germany, that were in excessive deficit. In purely economic terms, though, the original stability pact was too rigid, pushing countries into pro-cyclical austerity whenever they found themselves in a downturn. The reformed version made greater allowances for the impact of the economic cycle, and tried to strip out one-off measures through which countries sought to game the numbers.

Most euro-zone countries remained within the limits and, in subsequent years, the number of sinners gradually declined. The real failing of the pact was that an obsession with budgets, especially the annual deficits, blinded ministers and officials to more serious underlying problems in the euro zone. "The whole system was looking at the economy through the keyhole of fiscal policy," says one Commission veteran. By 2007 the fiscal situation had seemingly never been better. All members of the euro zone were out of the excessive deficit procedure (EDP) by mid-2008, and so formally deemed to have their public finances in order though the credit crunch was intensifying. The Commission boasted that reform of the pact had promoted discipline and national "ownership". Even Greece was released from the EDP in 2007, despite persistent doubts about the reliability of its figures. But, rather as with the enforcement of the pact, governments would not hear of the Commission being given the power to audit their national figures.

It is significant that, on the eve of the crisis, three of the five countries that would later have to be bailed out – Ireland, Spain and Cyprus – were virtuous by the standards of the stability and growth pact. They were running budget surpluses and had a stock of debt well below the Maastricht ceiling of 60% of GDP. Their problem was not a matter of poor enforcement, or of fabricated statistics, but of a misguided belief that controlling fiscal policy was all that really mattered. The crisis revealed the much greater importance of several other factors: economic imbalances, particularly in the current account of the balance of payments; private debt; and the role of the financial sector in financing external deficits.

Unbalanced

The focus on fiscal rules had been justified by two beliefs. The first was that, in a single currency with a common exchange rate and monetary policy, fiscal sinners were less likely to be punished by markets that might otherwise speculate against a country in danger of running into problems of high inflation or debt. Profligacy in one country could thus drive up borrowing costs for all. The second, conversely, was that a euro-zone country that got into trouble would not be able to devalue or loosen monetary policy, and would not enjoy the sorts of automatic transfers that operate in federal countries, so the main tool to absorb a shock would be greater borrowing by the government: hence the need for sound public finances.

In countries with their own currencies, markets and policymakers closely watch the current account for signs of an economy getting out of line. The current-account balance is a measure of the balance of trade, foreign income and transfers. A deficit can be a problem if, say, it highlights a country's loss of competitiveness and export share; or it can be benign, if it reflects greater returns on capital flowing into a country undergoing a period of fast catch-up growth. Current-account deficits must by definition be financed by capital inflows. Yet there was a widespread belief, echoed on occasion by the Commission and the ECB, that, in a single-currency zone with an integrated financial market, current-account imbalances did not matter any more than they did within federal countries like the United States.

In the early 2000s, years that became known as the "great moderation", when money was cheap, euro-zone countries were able to build up large external imbalances (15% of GDP in Greece). Had they still had national currencies, this would surely have provoked a response from markets. Instead, everybody benefited from low interest rates. Thus was born the great paradox of economic and monetary union. In order for countries to survive within it, they needed to make deeper structural reforms to improve their competitiveness; and yet the pressure to push through those reforms was reduced by the benign mood of financial markets. Many had hoped the creation of the euro would force ossified countries like Italy to change their ways. Losing the ability to devalue meant that competitiveness could be recovered only by "internal devaluation" (that is, bringing down wages and prices relative to others), boosting productivity, or both. This meant liberalising labour and product markets, and promoting competition. But for countries used to high inflation and high interest rates before the launch of the euro, any loss of competitiveness could be masked for a long time by cheaper money.

By about 2005 it was apparent that national economies, far from converging as they had been expected to do, were pulling apart. The differences were no greater than the dispersion in growth rates in

FIG 4.1 **From hares to tortoises**
GDP, 1999–2014, 1999 = 100

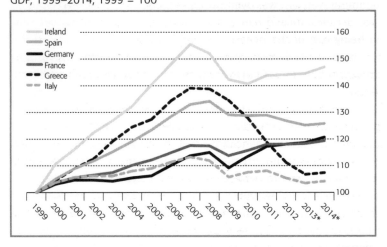

*Forecast
Source: Eurostat

American states, but they were worryingly persistent. Some were growing fast with high inflation, among them Ireland, Greece and Spain. All were enjoying a boom fuelled by low interest rates. At the other end of the spectrum, mighty Germany was growing anaemically, but with very low inflation. To some extent the ECB's one-size-fits-all interest rate exacerbated this polarisation: interest rates were too low for overheating countries, but too high for Germany (the situation is reversed today). The two oddities were Italy and Portugal, which seemed to be suffering the worst of both worlds with, simultaneously, slow growth and higher-than-average inflation (see Figure 4.1).

There were, indeed, marked differences among both the hares and the tortoises. Among the fast-growing countries, Greece had a government that was spending recklessly and fiddling statistics, whereas Spain and Ireland had public finances seemingly in good order, but private sectors that were running up high debt as a side-effect of housing booms. Too few questioned whether buoyant tax revenues might not just be a windfall from a property bubble. When it burst, they would collapse and spending would shoot up to pay for unemployed construction workers. Ireland's net exports were booming even as it was overheating, but Spain's were shrinking. Over two decades, Ireland had gone from being the poorest EU country to being one of the richest. But while the Celtic Tiger put on real muscle in the early years, boosting productivity by turning itself into an export base for multinationals, later it just gorged itself on cheap credit.

Among the laggards, Germany's sickliness masked a process of protracted reform, especially Gerhard Schröder's Agenda 2010 labour-market and welfare changes, pushed through after 2003. Germany was still digesting the cost of absorbing the former East Germany, and had entered the euro with an overvalued currency. But in a country accustomed to living with a hard currency and low inflation, and relatively consensual industrial relations, German bosses and workers set off on the long slog of wage restraint to regain competitiveness. Internal demand was so weak that almost all Germany's growth came from increasing exports. But in Italy and Portugal slow growth was an unmistakable signal of reform paralysis. Both were losing export share. Higher inflation was pushing up wages, while productivity was stagnant. Italy had higher debt than Portugal, but Portugal was running higher budget deficits.

One cause of the problem was that southern European countries were hit harder than northern ones by China's entry into the World Trade Organisation at the end of 2001. China's exports of textiles, clothing and footwear grew sharply; those of Italy and Portugal declined markedly. Another issue was that foreign direct investment had shifted from the Mediterranean countries to the new countries from central and eastern Europe which joined the EU in 2004. There cheap skilled labour was plentiful. Germany made full use of the opportunity by shifting factory production eastward. But France, among others, resisted. Rather it regarded low-cost, low-tax eastern Europe resentfully as a source of competition and "social dumping". According to the World Bank, which in 2012 produced a detailed report on Europe's economic model,[1] another drawback in southern Europe was that many of its small family-run businesses were unsuited to competing in a big European market.

The striking north–south divide that has emerged in Europe may

have even more profound historical and sociological roots. Many cite
Max Weber's Protestant work ethic. Others speak of Catholics' greater
readiness to absolve sins. When giving lectures, Vítor Constâncio,
vice-president of the ECB and a former economics professor from
Portugal, would sometimes hold up a colour-coded map of Europe
and ask audiences what the darker colours in the north and lighter
shades in the south might represent. The usual reply was GDP per
head. In fact, they denoted literacy rates in the 19th century, with
bible-reading northern Protestants more literate than the priest-
dominated southern Catholics. Plainly debt and deficits are not the
only or even the best measure of economic health. The trend in unit
labour costs (flat in Germany but rising fast in the periphery) and
current-account balances (surpluses in Germany and deficits in the
periphery) is crucial.

Some of the euro zone's problems might have been alleviated
by reforms, both national and European, to make wages and prices
more responsive. But along with reform fatigue in member countries,
there was also integration fatigue across the EU. Deepening the single
market might have provided a source of growth and competitive
impulse. Much of the EU's productivity lag, in comparison with
the United States, is due to underperforming services. But the EU's
services directive, designed to break down some of the barriers,
was watered down after the defeat of the constitutional treaty in
referendums in France and the Netherlands in 2005. One reason
was the panic in France over the supposed threat of the "Polish
plumber". Soon afterwards Roberto Maroni, an Italian minister from
the Northern League, caused a stir by excoriating the euro for Italy's
poor performance and calling for a return to the lira.

Slow growth, economic divergence and political tension led some
economists to start asking as early as 2006 whether the euro might
break apart. Daniel Gros of the Centre for European Policy Studies,
a think-tank in Brussels, thought that sluggish Germany and roaring
Spain would soon swap places (he also worried about Italy).[2] Simon
Tilford of the Centre for European Reform in London painted a
scenario in which markets might lose confidence in Italy, with its slow
growth and reluctance to reform, pushing up its borrowing costs and
debt, in turn prompting demands that Italy leave the euro.[3]

Banking on the euro

The launch of the euro greatly increased financial integration. Often banks grew large in comparison to their home countries' GDP, and in comparison to banks in the United States, in part because European firms relied more heavily on bank loans than on the corporate-bond market. But it was a lopsided sort of integration. Cross-border lending to banks and sovereigns grew fast, but retail lending remained Balkanised in national markets. Cross-border ownership of banks grew only slowly. Mergers and acquisitions tended to happen within a country's borders, a sign of strong economic nationalism in the banking sector.

Cross-border ownership was most apparent in the EU's new members from central and eastern Europe. Among members of "old" Europe it remained for the most part tiny. But by late 2007, partly as a result of the Commission's efforts to chip away at internal barriers, there was enough cross-border expansion to prompt at least one economist, Nicolas Véron, to publish a paper for the Bruegel think-tank in Brussels titled: *Is Europe Ready for a Major Banking Crisis?*[4] He noted that banks had become too large and diversified for national supervisors, even if they met in the then Committee of European Banking Supervisors (CEBS), to oversee properly. He said:

> The prudential framework for pan-European banks has become
> a maze of national authorities (51 are members of CEBS alone),
> EU-level committees (no fewer than nine) and bilateral arrangements
> (some 80 recently mentioned by European Commissioner Charlie
> McCreevy).

In an early hint at the future "banking union" that would emerge five years later, Véron argued that the largest cross-border banks (including British ones, given London's large financial centre) should be supervised by an EU-level body, with a single set of rules to deal with failing banks and a harmonised deposit-insurance system.

Financial integration, it was widely hoped, would stimulate a more efficient allocation of capital across the EU. And in the euro zone, it was supposed to provide a means of absorbing country-specific shocks given the lack of adjustment tools. But when crisis struck, financial integration provided an open channel for financial contagion to spread. The fact that banks were large, and that their bond holdings were strongly biased in favour of their own sovereign's debt, helped create a deadly feedback loop between weak sovereigns and weak banks. And because most of the banks' cross-border assets were in the form of lending, rather than equity, the international flows that had financed euro-zone imbalances could more easily be cut off when credit became scarce.

Resounding complacency

Most or all of these problems were reasonably well understood and, indeed, predicted before the launch of the euro. In the Commission's book on the euro, EMU@10,[5] published in 2008 just ahead of the tenth anniversary of the start of the monetary union, there is mention of worries about imbalances, the divergence of economies and the dangers lurking in the banking system. But nowhere in its 320 turgid pages did it issue a clear warning, of the sort that some independent economists were voicing, about the risks of a self-fulfilling market panic, or of a destructive doom-loop between banks and sovereigns, or of large contingent liabilities in banks ending up on the books of already overindebted sovereigns. The clearest message was one of self-congratulation over the "resounding success" of the euro. It had boosted economic stability, cross-border trade, financial integration and investment, declared the authors. Traumatic exchange-rate crises were a thing of the past, and fiscal stability had been enhanced. Indeed, the euro had become "a pole of stability for Europe and the world economy". The euro having survived a decade, and regained its strength against the dollar, it was perhaps natural for European officials to boast of its achievements and dismiss the doomsayers, particularly those from the English-speaking world.

A much deeper mystery is the complacency of financial markets. They utterly failed to distinguish between the dodgy credit of Greece and the rock-solid dependability of Germany. The yield on government bonds (which moves inversely to price) fell in peripheral countries in the early years of the euro so that it became almost identical across the euro zone. Italy sometimes had to pay six percentage points more

FIG 4.2 **Unbonded**
Ten-year bond yields, 1995–2010, %

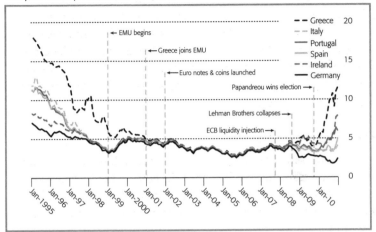

Source: Eurostat

than Germany in interest to borrow money in the 1990s. By 2007, this "spread" had fallen to a fraction of a percentage point (about 20 basis points). Getting markets to impose discipline on governments had been one reason for enshrining the no-bail-out rule and forbidding the ECB from monetising government debt.

Perhaps investors were simply chasing anything that offered a marginally better yield. Markets often overshoot in both directions, after all. Some were still convinced the euro would lead to convergence among European economies. Others assumed that default within the euro zone was unthinkable: whatever the treaties said, solidarity among members would prevail, one way or another. In his 1989 report on setting up a single currency, Jacques Delors himself had argued that, far from penalising imbalances, financial markets might for a while finance them because of the attraction of a large pool of euro-denominated debt:[6]

Rather than leading to gradual adaptation of borrowing costs, market views about the creditworthiness of official borrowers tend to change abruptly and result in the closure of access to market financing.

As Figure 4.2 on page 37 shows, bond yields of countries in the euro zone between 1990 and 2010 thus came to look like a length of rope frayed at both ends. Before EMU yields were spread far apart, reflecting the market's perception of each country's risk of inflation, devaluation and default. They then narrowed as the launch of EMU approached before becoming closely entwined through the first decade of the euro. Then, with the onset of the euro crisis in late 2008, they spread out once more as markets suddenly started to worry about the risk of default. Greece and Ireland were to be the first strands to come loose.

5 Trichet's test

OF THE SENIOR FIGURES IN THE EURO ZONE, it was Jean-Claude Trichet, president of the European Central Bank, who gave the clearest warnings of the danger of growing deficits. He was a hawk about respecting the stability and growth pact. Moreover, from 2005, he would turn up every month at ministerial meetings with charts setting out his concerns about economic imbalances. A favourite one showed the divergence in unit labour costs across the euro zone. Another tracked the giddy rise of public-sector wages. His main concern was that the loss of competitiveness would harm growth. But he also knew the euro zone was not a federal country; there was no central budget to help countries that got into trouble. The countries of the euro zone, he would say, were like *La Cigale et la Fourmi*, Jean de la Fontaine's fable about the improvident cicada and the hard-working ant. Those in the periphery sang in the warm sunshine, while the industrious Germans held down their wages and put money aside for a rainy day. But when winter came, Trichet could scarcely stand aside. Central banks wield the power of financial alchemy, able to produce an endless quantity of money out of thin air. Often only the ECB had the means to provide the vast amounts of liquidity needed to stop a run on sound banks, or on solvent sovereigns.

The ECB's treaty-prescribed independence gives it a peculiarly remote, Olympian status. In public, the dialogue between governments and the central bank is detached and reverential. Governments are frowned upon if they demand action from the ECB too vehemently in public. Behind the scenes, the ECB has been an intensely political actor, from designing and monitoring bail-out programmes to engaging in hand-to-hand combat with leaders over reforms. The Gallic rows between Trichet and the French president, Nicolas Sarkozy, became legendary. Of the ECB's component banks, Germany's Bundesbank is the most important and pure in its conviction that it is not the job of central bankers to get politicians out of fiscal trouble. Its president, Jens Weidmann, believes the ECB should act like Odysseus before the sirens: lash itself to the mast with strict rules and tell the sailors to stuff their ears with wax to shut out the politicians' calls. This is the backdrop to the crisis as it developed from 2007.

Chacun sa merde

As global credit dried up after the collapse of subprime mortgages in the United States, the ECB was the first to open the cash tap on August 9th 2007, making an extra €95 billion available to banks, soon followed by the central banks of the United States, Canada, Japan and Australia. The trigger was the announcement that BNP Paribas, a French bank, was suspending withdrawals from two funds heavily exposed to subprime credit. It said a shortage of liquidity made the assets impossible to value. Any doubts that Europe would feel the force of the financial crisis were quickly dispelled. A few days earlier IKB, a German bank that had played recklessly with asset-backed investments, had been bailed out; a month later there was a run on Northern Rock, a British lender that would eventually be nationalised. Trichet's quick and firm response prompted the *Financial Times* to pick him in December 2007 as its "Person of the Year".

It was the bankruptcy of Lehman Brothers on September 15th 2008 that really caused global panic. The decision by Ireland a fortnight later to extend an unlimited guarantee to all banking debt provoked both anger at a rash move that was sucking deposits from the rest of Europe and a scramble by other countries to issue their own guarantees. Sarkozy, whose country held the rotating presidency of the EU, sought to control the free-for-all by calling a summit of leaders of the four biggest European economies on October 4th. He pushed for the creation of a common European bank-rescue fund, worth perhaps €300 billion, but was slapped down by Angela Merkel, the German chancellor. "*Elle a dit, chacun sa merde*" ("she said everybody should deal with his own shit") was how Sarkozy scathingly recounted the conversation to his aides. At another summit in Paris eight days later, this time of all euro-zone leaders plus the UK's prime minister, Gordon Brown, Merkel changed her tune. Her mind concentrated by the collapse between the two summits of Hypo Real Estate, she now accepted the need for a massive European response. It would be worth €1.9 trillion in loan guarantees and capital injections to prop up the banks. The move was co-ordinated and subject to EU state-aid rules, but each country would still have to clean up its own banking mess. The hyperactive Sarkozy then flew off to Camp David (taking along the president of the European Commission, José Manuel Barroso) to persuade President George Bush to call a global summit on the financial crisis (it would become the G20 summit).

Under the Irish single-market commissioner, Charlie McCreevy, the Commission had hitherto favoured light-touch regulation of finance. But in October Barroso enlisted a former IMF boss and French central-bank governor, Jacques de Larosière, to produce a report on how to tighten control over the financial sector. It was delivered within three months. After much resistance from the UK, the report would lead to the creation in 2011 of four new European financial supervisory bodies: three new regulators for banks, insurance and markets, and the European Systemic Risk Board to monitor threats to the overall financial system. The task would be pursued with zeal after 2010 by McCreevy's French successor, Michel Barnier, who vowed that no aspect of finance would escape regulation.

Soon after Lehman's demise, staff at the IMF's European department predicted that "it's going to rain programmes". The first came in the form of a classic balance-of-payments crisis that hit the newer, fast-growing eastern EU members that were outside the euro. As foreign money fled and currencies came under pressure, Hungary and then Latvia applied for IMF bail-outs in October and December 2008, respectively. Romania followed in March 2009. These bail-outs were co-financed by the EU, the World Bank and others. The eastern turmoil fed the illusion that the euro had brought protection from the worst of the crisis. Trichet called the single currency "a shield" against global turbulence. Slovakia was more than glad to be able to slip into the single currency on January 1st 2009. To the fury of some, the euro zone resisted pressure to soften its admission criteria so that others could follow.

But the combined impact of bank rescues, fiscal stimulus and the start of recession aggravated the public finances of several countries. Might the crisis spread to the euro zone after all? Ireland and Cyprus were likely candidates for assistance because of their outsized banking sectors. Spain looked fragile because of its property bust. Others thought that Austria was vulnerable because of its banks' exposure to central and eastern Europe. However, the first euro-zone debt crisis would begin in a country whose banks were reasonably sound, but whose public spending had run out of control and whose statistics were dodgy: Greece.

Greek tragedy

Oddly, perhaps, the first blow to Greek debt was not financial but political. The death of a 15-year-old schoolboy, shot by the police in December 2008, set off a fortnight of riots across the country. Even for people used to a degree of ritualised street clashes, the scale of the unrest was unprecedented since the restoration of democracy in 1974. The violence seemed to reflect a deep malaise over high youth unemployment, a dynastic political system based on patronage, a kleptocratic and ineffective public administration, educational reforms – and the public bail-out of banks. Other European leaders worried that the rebelliousness might spread (Sarkozy cancelled a planned school reform, fearing "regicidal" mobs).

The teetering Greek prime minister, Kostas Karamanlis, sacked his finance minister, George Alogoskoufis, a month later and then loosened the public purse-strings ahead of an election. Greek bond yields had been drifting upward from the start of the credit crunch in 2007. But with the riots the spread over German bonds blew out, rising from about 160 to 300 basis points in late January 2009, after Standard & Poor's had downgraded Greece's debt. The European Commission placed Greece (and five others) under surveillance for breaching the 3% deficit limit. It said Greece and Ireland should step up deficit-cutting.

Senior French and German officials held secret meetings about how to respond should Greece lose access to bond markets. But the problem seemed to resolve itself, helped by reassurances from the

German finance minister, Peer Steinbrück, that weaker euro-zone members would be helped if they got into trouble. The comments were echoed by the Commission and the ECB. For a while the unspoken assumption that countries of the euro zone would stand behind each other in case of trouble appeared to have been reaffirmed. Spreads narrowed again. Then the Greek Socialist opposition party, Pasok, won a landslide victory in the election on October 4th 2009. Its leader, George Papandreou, son and grandson of previous Greek prime ministers, had campaigned on a policy of fiscal stimulus. He had promised above-inflation pay rises, investment in green energy and other spending to "kick the economy back into action again". Output was at a standstill because of a drop in summer tourism and shipping revenues had fallen because of shrinking global trade. But Papandreou breezily declared that "the money exists".

It didn't. On October 16th, less than a fortnight after coming to power, Papandreou announced that the previous government had left an enormous hole in the budget. His finance minister, George Papaconstantinou, said the deficit for 2010 would be above 10% of GDP, a figure promptly revised up to 12.7%. Yet surprisingly, fellow European leaders at first paid little attention to this opening act of the Greek tragedy. Policy debate focused on financial regulation, how to end stimulus programmes amid signs of a tentative recovery and the conclusion of the long saga of the Lisbon treaty. An EU summit in November did not even discuss Greece, but rather who should fill the two big jobs created by the treaty: the eventual choices were Herman Van Rompuy as European Council president and Catherine Ashton as foreign-policy chief. Meanwhile, as ratings agencies downgraded Greece, finance ministers chastised the country. At a summit in December Papandreou delivered an unusually candid admission of Greek corruption before fellow leaders. Yet many still hoped that Greece would somehow get itself out of trouble by tightening its belt.

Solvay doesn't solve it

Van Rompuy's inaugural act was to call an informal summit at the Bibliothèque Solvay in Brussels on February 11th 2010 to hold a general debate on the EU's growth-promotion strategy. But as Greek bond yields spiked over the 7% mark in late January, he realised something would have to be done, or at least said. Van Rompuy had little idea how much his presidency would be dominated by the Greek crisis. But his mild, self-deprecating manner – and his experience as Belgium's budget minister in bringing down his country's debt – made him an ideal backroom dealmaker. He delayed the start of the summit for more than two hours, closeting himself with Papandreou, the leaders of France, Germany, the European Commission and the ECB. The previous year French and German officials had spoken privately of extending bilateral lines of credit should Greece get into trouble, but the German coalition had since changed and the public mood was hostile to any idea of lending money. Germans had been promised they would never have to pay for other countries. Perversely, perhaps, it was easier to help non-euro EU countries in financial trouble than to lend money to the likes of Greece.

From the outset the discussion reflected national prejudices and personal traits that would shape the subsequent response. The imperious Sarkozy wanted European leaders to react quickly and forcefully; the cautious Merkel was in no rush to respond. The former thought the crisis would go away if governments just put up enough money to see off the speculators; the latter was convinced that the crisis would be assuaged if Greece just took serious action to cut its deficit and reform its economy. In a country that had not run a budget surplus since 1974, French voters did not share the same resentment as German ones over Greek profligacy. Sarkozy also rejected the involvement of the IMF as an affront to Europe. Trichet concurred, perhaps also because he thought the IMF would try to impose conditions on the ECB. Both men may have been conscious that the IMF was run by Dominique Strauss-Kahn, a potential Socialist challenger to Sarkozy. Yet after sharing these initial qualms, Germany came round to insisting on IMF involvement to ensure rigour.

Van Rompuy papered over these differences with a statement that declared support for Greece "to do whatever is necessary" to curb its deficit, and announced that the Commission would "monitor" the implementation of the promised deficit-cutting, "drawing on the expertise of the IMF". He said euro-zone members "will take determined and co-ordinated action, if needed, to safeguard financial stability in the euro area as a whole". But to get Merkel to swallow the implicit commitment to a bail-out, he added a final sentence: "The Greek government has not requested any financial support."

Irrational *ultima ratio*

By March everybody knew the request would come. The "troika" that would negotiate the bail-out – consisting of the IMF, the European Commission and the ECB – was born and made an initial secret visit to Greece in early March. Amid ugly German headlines telling Greeks to "sell your islands" and a magazine cover depicting Venus de Milo giving Europe the middle finger, a summit on March 25th prepared what Greece called a "loaded gun". Member countries declared that they stood ready to pool bilateral loans into a fund that, along with the IMF, was ready to bail out Greece. Germany attached several conditions: a decision had to be taken unanimously and include "strong conditionality" to reform, and loans would be extended at "non-concessional" interest rates, reflecting the risk of lending to Greece. Above all, the mechanism could be used only on the basis of *ultima ratio*, as a last resort to prevent Greece from defaulting on its debt. This German doctrine, born of tactical, domestic and legal considerations, would come repeatedly to hamper the euro zone's ability to respond decisively.

Germany believed, with good reason, that countries would cut their budget deficits and reform their economies only under extreme pressure from markets. Moreover, Merkel could hope to win over her outraged voters to the idea of a bail-out only if she could demonstrate that it was needed to save the euro. And given that opponents would inevitably petition the constitutional court in Karlsruhe, she could justify the breach of the no-bail-out rule in European treaties only on the grounds of a genuine emergency, on the well-known principle of *Not kennt kein Gebot*: "Necessity knows no law". Lawyers in Brussels also noted that the no-bail-out rule was hardly categorical. The Lisbon treaty says only that countries that shall "not be liable for or assume" the debt of others; it says nothing of lending money.[1] That the euro zone would later invoke another article dealing with assistance for natural disasters says much about the legal discomfort.[2]

The loaded gun did not frighten the markets. The Eurogroup then cocked the weapon on April 11th, saying that it stood ready to lend Greece €30 billion in the first year of a programme, to which the IMF would add another €15 billion. A premium of 300 basis points would be added to the borrowing costs – a steep price, but not as steep as the 7% yield that markets were demanding for Greek ten-year bonds. This still provided no deterrent. In late April Standard & Poor's downgraded Greek debt to junk status, and also cut its ratings for Portuguese and Spanish bonds. On May 2nd, responding to a formal request for help from Papandreou, who said his country was "a sinking ship", the Eurogroup agreed to the inevitable bail-out. It had grown to €110 billion over three years – the largest ever provided to a single country – as it became obvious that private investors would not roll over existing debt.

Even so, the deal was filled with contradictions. Greece was supposedly being rescued, but it was subjected to an unworkable programme and punitive rates of interest (Merkel boasted that Germany would make a profit on the loans). IMF staff thought there should be less up-front austerity and more structural reforms, but the Europeans were still focused on fiscal rules. The debt-sustainability assessment relied on optimistic assumptions. One IMF official was blunter: "We lied." Indeed, it would emerge later that many members of the IMF's board had deep misgivings about the programme.[3] Brazil's executive director, Paulo Nogueira Batista, was prescient when he argued that the risks of the programme were immense. Rather than a bail-out of Greece it could become a bail-out of investors and banks as they dumped their bonds onto official lenders. The whole thing could prove "ill conceived and ultimately unsustainable". Critics argued that Greece's huge debt should instead have been restructured immediately. That said, even the most hawkish IMF staff members thought it was too dangerous to do this in the middle of a market panic. But the lingering dispute would, later on, harden the IMF's attitude to Greece and future rescues.

Even the tripling of the Greek bail-out failed to quell the markets. And the crippling adjustment demanded of Greece – deficit reduction of 11 percentage points over three years in the teeth of a recession, nearly half of it front-loaded in the first year – provoked riots outside the Greek parliament, and the death of three people when anarchists set fire to a bank. As Greek bonds rose beyond 12%, contagion pushed Irish yields close to 6% and Portuguese ones up above 7%. Stockmarkets around the world slumped as investors fretted about the financial and political stability of a block that made up around a quarter of global output.

Save the euro

After months of indecision and half measures, the euro was now in mortal danger. The mood of foreboding grew darker still on May 6th 2010, the day of a strange "flash-crash" on Wall Street, in which the Dow Jones Industrial Average collapsed by about 1,000 points before recovering within minutes, perhaps because of a technical glitch. The ECB's governing council, in Lisbon that day for its monthly meeting, faced a momentous decision: should it start buying sovereign bonds to stop the panic? The Federal Reserve and the Bank of England had been doing so under their policy of quantitative easing to bring down long-term borrowing costs. But the ECB had not gone so far, wary of the prohibition against anything resembling "monetary financing", that is, printing money to finance public debt. After the official meeting, Trichet told journalists that the subject of bond-buying had not been discussed. Later on over an informal dinner, however, the council had reached a tentative agreement to start selectively buying the bonds of vulnerable countries.[4] The next day, as leaders gathered in Brussels for a euro-zone-only summit, ostensibly to endorse the bail-out of Greece, many participants seemed unaware that they would be called upon to do something much bigger: set up a safety net for the whole euro zone.

Trichet delivered a stern lecture. He told leaders the euro was in danger, and that they were to blame for the mess through reckless policies. It was now their responsibility to fix it. Trichet would not disclose his readiness to buy bonds until the leaders had taken decisive action; the ECB would not risk acting alone, or being seen to do so under political pressure. The summit could not reach agreement, so finance ministers were told to take up the task two days later, a Sunday, before markets reopened in Asia. The Commission then tabled a proposal, based on its aid programme for central and eastern Europe, to create a €60 billion war chest for the euro zone. The money would be raised by issuing bonds on the market guaranteed by the EU budget. The British prime minister, Gordon Brown, who had just lost a general election on May 6th, had to be asked for his approval. Member countries, including the non-euro UK, would be liable for possible losses.

Yet too little money could be raised this way. And ministers would not extend loan guarantees to the Commission to expand the fund. Instead, a special-purpose company, incorporated in Luxembourg and backed by government guarantees, would be created to ensure national governments retained full control over the money. The final deal could not be concluded until nightfall, after polling stations closed in the German state of North-Rhine Westphalia (Merkel's Christian Democrats lost). Consensus was then quickly reached on the amount: €440 billion. Thus were born the Commission's European Financial Stabilisation Mechanism (EFSM) and the larger inter-governmental European Financial Stability Facility (EFSF). The IMF would match every two euros put up by the euro zone with one of its own, an unusual entry into rich-world affairs. The total made available to defend the euro zone amounted to €750 billion, or roughly a round $1 trillion.

Trichet now had the political cover he needed. The ECB announced that it would buy bonds under the Securities Market Programme (SMP), not to help crippled countries but on the grounds that dysfunctional markets were "hampering the monetary policy transmission mechanism". At the same time, the ECB opened the tap for liquidity to the banks, while the Federal Reserve and other central banks helped out by reopening dollar swap lines, in essence a means for the Federal Reserve to extend dollar liquidity in the global financial system via other countries' central banks (which would continue to bear the credit risk). The enormous sums mobilised that weekend were supposed to be a deterrent, a weapon never to be used. But, just as with the "big bazooka" that Hank Paulson, then the American treasury secretary, had talked about in 2008, it would not be long before it had to be deployed.

The ECB's U-turn on bond-buying, following an earlier U-turn on taking Greek bonds as collateral for banks, raised questions about its independence. Tellingly, Merkel gave the bank the nod to buy bonds even though Axel Weber, the Bundesbank president, who briefly flirted with the idea, opposed the move. It is easier for politicians to have the central bank put up the money than ask for it from taxpayers. Moreover, governments could not make up their minds about markets. They denounced speculators for plotting to destroy the euro, yet set out to borrow hundreds of billions from the same financiers to save the single currency. They blamed ratings agencies for ignoring the dangers of dodgy financial engineering, then excoriated them for exaggerating the threat of sovereign default. But the events in May established one principle: faced with catastrophe, governments would act. The ECB would act too, though only if governments moved first. Yet delay raised the price of resolving the crisis, and also fed doubts about whether the euro could survive.

Merkozy in Deauville

The European summits in June and September 2010 were more or less routine affairs, although spreads started creeping up again in the summer after the market euphoria in May. Governments turned to reforming the institutional set-up of the euro. Part of the price Merkel demanded for bailing out Greece was a strengthening of the stability and growth pact, and closer co-ordination of economic policies to improve the competitiveness of the weaker countries. This became part of her mantra: greater control in exchange for greater solidarity. Sarkozy was not keen on such notions. But he liked the idea of creating a smaller, more exclusive core club that would keep out pesky liberal free traders from the UK and other north European countries. In March Sarkozy had started pushing an old French concept of an economic "government" for the euro zone, later softened in official communiqués as "governance". To his mind, economies should be run by leaders with lots of discretion, not by rule-bound bureaucrats. One undeclared aim was to restrain competition by harmonising taxes and social spending to French levels.

Reconciling these positions was made harder by two problems. First, the Franco-German relationship, the traditional engine of European integration, was working poorly. Second, both Sarkozy and Merkel were deeply suspicious of the European Commission. So in March 2010 EU leaders appointed Van Rompuy, not Barroso, the Commission president, to draw up a plan to toughen fiscal rules. But the Commission then pre-empted Van Rompuy's report by publishing its own package of six legislative proposals on economic governance (later known as the "six-pack"). Beyond deficits, the six-pack put greater emphasis on reducing the stock of debt (to Italy's dismay). And beyond the fiscal targets, EU surveillance would look at a broader range of economic indicators to detect underlying imbalances. Lastly, it inverted voting rules so that sanctions against miscreants no longer required a qualified majority of countries; instead, penalties recommended by the Commission would be approved unless blocked by a qualified majority.

Germany also pushed two more radical ideas. One was to suspend the voting rights of profligate countries. Such provisions existed for countries breaching fundamental values of democracy and human rights; the same should apply for breaches of the euro zone's fiscal rules, thought Merkel. Her other demand was a mechanism for the "orderly insolvency" of governments. This idea was not new. After Argentina's default on its foreign debt in 2001, the IMF proposed a statutory "sovereign debt restructuring mechanism", an insolvency regime for governments akin to the US Chapter 11 bankruptcy for companies. The aim was to make default less messy and painful, and ensure that bail-outs do not serve just a few lucky creditors. But the proposal ran into insurmountable opposition, not least from the United States, which did not want to cede power to a supranational authority to co-ordinate the process. The crisis in Greece brought the idea back to the fore. In the euro zone, at least, the idea of a supranational body was well-established though at times accepted only grudgingly.

All this was part of Germany's determined effort to minimise the risk that it would be called upon again to bail out another country or, indeed, to bail out Greece a second time. Tougher fiscal rules, monitoring and sanctions would reduce the chances of countries getting into trouble. And if another debt crisis did take place, and the country needed a bail-out, the taxpayer should not be made to carry the whole burden. Moreover, the threat of losses should sharpen the vigilance of bond markets.

Other countries for the most part accepted the need to strengthen the stability and growth pact. But governments, and above all the ECB, were resistant to any notion of facilitating debt restructuring. One reason was a reluctance to bear the stigma: defaulting on debt was something that happened in poorer countries, not the industrialised world. Another was a concern that, in a world in which countries could more easily restructure debt, the borrowing costs for all sovereigns might be raised. A third was the fear of rekindling market turbulence. Instead of ensuring that markets enforced discipline on governments in future, debt restructuring might prompt another panic that would push governments into immediate bankruptcy. After all, Greece was not the only European country with a large burden of debt.

Some of the changes that Germany demanded would require a change of the treaties, which many countries were reluctant to embark on after the political agony they suffered over the constitutional and Lisbon treaties. But Merkel favoured treaty change anyway, despite the promise that Lisbon would be the last revision in a generation. She worried that the legal basis of the EFSF might not stand up to challenge in the Karlsruhe court. Even if it did, the fund was due to expire in 2013 and would surely have to be replaced by something more permanent.

On October 18th Van Rompuy called a last meeting of his taskforce of finance ministers in Luxembourg. Christine Lagarde, then the French finance minister, predictably sought to amend the "automaticity" of the sanctions. But all were astounded to hear the then German deputy finance minister, Jörg Asmussen, declare he was in complete agreement with her. What were France and Germany up to? The answer came later in the evening from the French seaside resort of Deauville, where Sarkozy was hosting Merkel for a Franco-German summit (as well as a three-way summit with Russia). France and Germany now supported a new treaty to make possible the creation of a "robust and permanent" crisis-resolution system. Germany got a promise that, in future bail-outs, there should be an "adequate participation by the private sector"; in other words, private bondholders would have to bear part of the pain in future crises. France obtained a softening of the "automatic" sanctions.

In Brussels the accord was seen as the worst of political deals. Many worried about the weakening of the commitment to fiscal discipline and feared that the threat of future debt restructuring, known as private-sector involvement (PSI), might cause alarm in markets that seemed to be calming down. Even Sarkozy's senior advisers warned him against it. They worried that the implicit assumption of solidarity within the euro zone was being explicitly rejected through PSI, with unforeseeable consequences. But he overruled them.

Deauville thus marks the start of the "Merkozy" era. Merkel became the dominant figure in Europe while Sarkozy decided that the only way to manage the crisis, and to keep markets off France's back, was to hug her close. Deauville also marked a second, more dangerous phase of the story. Investors started to walk away from vulnerable sovereigns and, within days, to run after a spate of bad news. A statistical revision raised Greece's 2009 deficit above 15% of GDP, and its overall debt by about 12 percentage points to 127% of GDP; Greece admitted it was having problems collecting taxes; and PIMCO, one of the biggest fixed-income managers, predicted that Greece was likely to default within three years.

The mood at the next EU summit on October 28th was grim. Leaders of smaller countries were annoyed by the Franco-German diktat and the pressure to reopen the treaties. And Trichet, who had demanded that the Van Rompuy report formally note his reservations over weakened sanctions, warned leaders over dinner that the threat of debt restructuring would spook markets. "You don't realise the gravity of the situation," began Trichet. But he was cut off by Sarkozy: "Perhaps you speak to bankers. We, we are answerable to our citizens." Merkel joined in: taxpayers could not be asked to foot the whole bill, not when they had just paid to save the banks. And Merkel got most of what she wanted, with surprising ease. The summit agreed to revise the treaty although, to make sure it was a "limited" change that could be passed with a smaller risk of referendums, Merkel had to abandon the demand to suspend voting rights, which Sarkozy had conceded at Deauville.

The euro zone thus abruptly moved from the idea of bailing out debtor countries to bailing in bondholders. The principle was sound but the execution contradictory, not least because, as explained initially by the Germans, PSI was likely to apply to all future bailouts. In May governments had declined to impose haircuts on Greek bonds for fear of destabilising markets, thus pretending that Greece's insolvency was merely a matter of a shortage of liquidity. Now they seemed to be threatening all future investors in euro-zone bonds with possible losses; in other words, even countries with liquidity problems might be treated as insolvent. For Trichet this was a betrayal of the ECB's politically risky decision to start buying government bonds to hold down borrowing costs. By the time of the G20 summit in Seoul on November 12th, yields on Portuguese and Irish bonds were well over their previous peaks in May. European finance ministers said the issue had been misunderstood: existing bonds were safe; only new bonds issued from 2013 might be subject to haircuts. But the damage of Deauville was done.

No luck for the Irish (or Portuguese)

Alarm now focused on Ireland. Having already poured billions into the banks, the government announced in September 2010 its "final estimate" for bank losses. Anglo Irish Bank, the most cavalier of the lot, would cost €30 billion. Added to Ireland's already large budget gap, the one-off cost of the banking bust pushed Ireland's budget deficit in 2010 to 32% of GDP. Fears for the solvency of the state pushed up bond yields. Deauville made a bad situation impossible. In mid-November Ireland started negotiating the terms for a bail-out, despite protests that it had enough cash to survive for months to come. But the ECB had had enough of propping up Irish banks. By the end of November Ireland had agreed to a €67.5 billion assistance package from the euro zone and the IMF, with bilateral loans from the UK and Sweden.

The liquidity provided by the ECB had proved to be a mixed blessing. It allowed Ireland to avoid a sudden stop in funding, as had previously happened in Iceland (which was not in the EU). But the ECB also prevented the Irish government from protecting taxpayers by imposing losses on senior bank creditors, again as had happened in Iceland (it also wiped out foreign depositors). Even so, the banking bust was not the only or even the main cause of Ireland's economic troubles; the recession caused by the bursting of the property bubble created a budget deficit of 12% of GDP in 2010. But the bad banks, and Deauville, tipped Ireland into seeking a bail-out. It also led to an early election and the fall of the Fianna Fail-led government of Brian Cowen in February 2011.

In Portugal, meanwhile, it was the resignation of the Socialist government of José Sócrates, which had failed to win parliamentary support for a fourth austerity budget in March 2011 that pushed the country into the arms of euro-zone rescuers. Portugal applied for a bail-out in April and finalised the negotiation for a €78 billion package on May 4th. Its debt was not as high as Greece's, nor did it have an out-of-control banking sector like Ireland. Instead, its woes were more like Italy's: years of chronically low growth. And whereas the euro zone had been reluctant to help Greece, it was now keen for both Ireland and Portugal to apply for assistance to try to stop contagion from spreading to bigger countries like Spain or Italy.

The programmes for Ireland and Portugal were devised with more plausible figures than the one for Greece. The two countries benefited from having fully functional governments and, especially in the case of Ireland, had export sectors that could benefit from the process of "internal devaluation". In contrast with Greece, moreover, both had opposition parties that for the most part agreed with the bail-out programmes. The election of Fine Gael's Enda Kenny in Ireland and of Pedro Passos Coelho of the Social Democratic Party in Portugal (both fiscal conservatives, despite the misleading name of the latter's party) caused little disruption to the troika's programme for fiscal consolidation and structural reforms.

Comprehensive failure

The new bail-outs in the winter of 2010–11 pushed European leaders to seek what they called a "comprehensive solution". There was, inevitably, much disagreement about what this would entail. Some thought the priority should be more "solidarity" to help countries cope with high bond yields. In December 2010 Jean-Claude Juncker, Luxembourg's veteran prime minister and president of the Eurogroup, co-authored a call with Italy's finance minister, Giulio Tremonti, for the euro zone to start issuing common Eurobonds, guaranteed jointly by all euro-zone countries. This would "send a clear message to global markets and European citizens of our political commitment to economic and monetary union, and the irreversibility of the euro".[5]

But Germany would have none of it. To begin with, joint bonds were illegal under the treaties, Germany argued. Moreover, guaranteeing the debt of others would mean taking on large and potentially unlimited liabilities, and would provide an incentive for profligacy. Instead, Germany wanted more control and discipline.

Its priority was the finalisation of the treaty change to create a permanent bail-out fund, to be known as the European Stability Mechanism (ESM). This was followed by moves to encourage more structural reforms. Over two summits in March 2011 leaders agreed to a voluntary pact to promote labour-market flexibility and other action. It was first known as the Competitiveness Pact, then the Pact for the Euro and, in its final form, the Euro Plus Pact. Once a year, countries would make reform commitments that would be scrutinised by peers. Some countries, like Belgium, disliked the challenge to their wage-indexation systems; others, like Ireland, worried about the pressure to raise their low corporate taxes. But perhaps the strongest reaction came from non-euro countries that disliked the commitment, pushed by France, to hold special euro-zone summits at least once a year. The Euro Plus Pact turned out to be ineffectual, and was soon forgotten. Many aspects of economic policy remained the competence of national governments, so the commitments would not be binding. A bit of peer pressure from Europe could not overcome the resistance at home that such reforms would inevitably provoke.

The question of solidarity could not be avoided for long. By spring it was apparent that the EFSF was underpowered, not just because it was starting to use up its resources for Ireland and Portugal, but because its real lending capacity was only about €250 billion, not the advertised €440 billion. Its ability to borrow on AAA terms was limited by the fact that only six countries had that credit rating. There was also growing pressure to turn the EFSF into a more flexible crisis-management tool, not just a fund of last resort. The "comprehensive package" announced on March 24th allowed both the temporary EFSF and the new ESM to buy bonds on the primary market (but not the secondary market). The ESM would not be operational until 2013. But the final agreement to enhance the EFSF, by increasing loan guarantees so that it could borrow to its full headline level, would have to wait until June, after an election in Finland.

On April 7th, the day that Portugal applied for its bail-out, the ECB decided perversely to raise its interest rate. The change was small – just 0.25% – but it was a wrong-headed signal nonetheless. Recovery in the euro zone was weak, with the notable exception of Germany. Headline inflation was slightly higher than the ECB's target of "below but close to 2%" because of higher oil prices, but core inflation was around 1%. The real argument was political. The ECB's bond-buying policy had prompted the resignation in February of Axel Weber, president of the Bundesbank and the most obvious successor to Trichet. It must have seemed a good moment for any hopefuls to establish their inflation-busting credentials.

Default options

By March 2011 the Greek problem was returning to the fore. Early on Papandreou had earned praise for some brave belt-tightening, but worries grew that structural reforms were falling behind and privatisation had made no progress at all. Matters were not helped by successive statistical revisions, which revealed Greece's fiscal hole to be deeper than expected. And the recession was also worse than expected. Behind closed doors at a summit on March 11th, Papandreou spoke about the grim options facing his country: leave the euro, impose haircuts on bondholders or change the market's perceptions.

A softening of the bail-out terms was an attempt to keep the third option alive: interest would be reduced by a point and loan maturities extended to 7.5 years (against a promise to step up privatisation). Ireland was denied the same terms because Kenny resisted pressure from Germany and especially France to raise its low rate of corporate tax, even though attracting investment and boosting exports offered the best hope of repaying its debt.

Despite the concession to Greece, the focus would quickly shift to debt restructuring. Talk at Deauville about PSI was pushing Greek bonds into a self-fulfilling spiral. Greek yields rose from mid-April amid growing talk of haircuts and even of Greece leaving the euro. Plainly, Greece would not be able to start borrowing from markets in 2012, as its bail-out programme projected. And unless the financing gap was filled, the IMF would have to suspend payments because of its rule that programmes be fully financed for a year in the future. The choice came down to granting Greece a second bail-out, belatedly restructuring its debt mountain, or some combination of the two. Germany and some IMF staff favoured imposing at least some losses on private bondholders. But they ran into two separate problems. The first was the arrest on charges of sexual assault (eventually dropped) of Strauss-Kahn, the IMF's chief. His deputy, John Lipsky, opposed debt restructuring; IMF hawks would have to bide their time until the arrival of Lagarde in July. The second and greater obstacle was the implacable resistance of the ECB to any of the various degrees of failure to repay debt fully and on time. No selective default, no credit event, no default, insisted Trichet; nothing should cast doubt on the "sovereign signature".

Greek politics also became more fraught. In June Papandreou replaced his finance minister, George Papaconstantinou, with Evangelos Venizelos, a party heavyweight. The new man made a poor impression at his first Eurogroup meeting when he insinuated that the euro zone could not afford to let Greece go bust.

No PSImple haircut

The summit in July 2011 turned into two separate negotiations, one among leaders and a parallel one with bankers, represented by the Institute of International Finance, for a "voluntary" contribution. After more than seven hours of talks, euro-zone leaders agreed to give Greece a second bail-out worth €109 billion. "Voluntary" PSI would bring in an extra €37 billion, resulting in an estimated cut of 21% in the debt burden (calculated in terms of net present value). The repayment terms on loans were greatly softened. The interest rate was brought down by another 150 basis points, to around 3.5%, and the maturities extended from 7.5 to between 15 and 30 years, with a ten-year grace period. Crucially, the same terms were extended to Ireland and Portugal, with a promise that the euro zone would continue to fund countries until they regained access to markets, as long as they complied with reform conditions. The decision proved to be a godsend for Ireland, whose bond yields progressively dropped, against the trend in southern Europe.

Leaders more or less buried Deauville when they declared that PSI had been an "an exceptional and unique" solution for Greece; all other countries would "honour fully their own individual sovereign signature". This had been one of three conditions set by Trichet in return for relenting on a limited debt restructuring. The others were that the ECB's holdings of Greek debt would be spared the haircut, and that the ESM would relieve the ECB of the burden of buying bonds on the secondary market. Indeed, the ESM was made more flexible in other ways too. It was also allowed to lend money to governments to recapitalise banks and extend precautionary loans.

The deal would prompt ratings agencies to declare a temporary "selective default" (the EFSF would have to offer the ECB alternative collateral), but its voluntary nature ensured it would not count as a "credit event" that triggered payments of credit-default swaps, a form of insurance against sovereign defaults. However, the deal proved to be the worst of both worlds: the haircut was too small to turn around Greece's public finances, but big enough to spread fear that other bonds were at risk.

Markets had other reasons to worry. The original banking crisis had never been satisfactorily resolved; it had only been masked by the Greek turmoil and, to a great extent, worsened by the sovereign-debt crisis. The second round of bank stress tests in July turned out to be another half-baked job. Plainly, sovereign bonds could no longer be treated as risk-free. But only the bonds in banks' trading books were accounted for at market value; those in the banking books were counted at face value because they would supposedly be held to maturity. Analysts derided the effort (only 9 out of 90 banks tested were found to require additional capital), but for senior officials, particularly in France, the tests already went too far in questioning the value of sovereign bonds. Even more alarming was a sharp warning by Lagarde, in her first speech as the new IMF chief, delivered at the annual central bankers' retreat in Jackson Hole at the end of August, when she called for mandatory recapitalisation of banks:

> *Banks need urgent recapitalisation. They must be strong enough to withstand the risks of sovereigns and weak growth. This is key to cutting the chains of contagion. If it is not addressed, we could easily*

see the further spread of economic weakness to core countries, or
even a debilitating liquidity crisis.

Night letters

In many ways, the euro crisis was always about Italy. A collapse of
the third-largest economy in the euro zone, and its second-largest
debtor in absolute terms, would surely sink the euro. Spain mattered
not only because it was larger than the other bailed-out states, but
also because it was the the last link in the chain of contagion before
Italy. The size of the euro zone's firewall was inadequate because it
could not protect Italy. Eurobonds were unacceptable because they
would mean Germany having to guarantee Italy's gargantuan debt.
And the fear of moral hazard was acute, in part because nobody
trusted Italian politicians to reform. Italy at least had the foresight not
to engage in fiscal stimulus, and its primary budget (that is, before
interest payments) was in surplus. Moreover, its banks seemed in
reasonable shape, and domestic savings were high. Even so, by the
start of August its borrowing costs had spiked above the 6% mark
(matched by Spain's yields). Everybody knew Italy was too big to
save. Only the ECB could help it stay afloat.

On August 5th 2011 Italy's prime minister, Silvio Berlusconi, received
a stern letter signed jointly by Trichet and Draghi. It urged him to take
"immediate and bold" measures to speed up Italy's deficit-cutting and
balance the budget by 2013, a year earlier than planned. It also set out
a list of "significant measures to enhance potential growth", including
the liberalisation of professional services and more labour-market
flexibility. In the longer term there had to be a constitutional reform
to enshrine fiscal rules, an overhaul of the public administration and
the abolition of costly layers of government. A similar letter was sent
to Spain's prime minister, José Luis Rodríguez Zapatero, though its
contents did not leak for two years.

A day earlier the ECB had revived its bond-buying programme,
initially only for Portugal and Ireland. The implied message was
clear: if Italy and Spain wanted help they had to reform fast, as if
they were under a troika programme. As the bank started buying up
unprecedented amounts of Spanish and Italian bonds, Jürgen Stark,

the German chief economist on the ECB's executive board, announced his resignation "for personal reasons": that is, his disapproval of bond-buying. Predictably enough, Berlusconi soon started watering down his proposed austerity budget, and did virtually nothing by way of structural reforms to accelerate Italy's sclerotic growth. His government was crumbling and his relationship with his finance minister, Giulio Tremonti, had all but broken down. On September 20th Standard & Poor's downgraded Italy, expressing doubt about its ability to reform. The ECB downgraded it silently, by sharply slowing down bond purchases. Amid mounting scandals over allegations of fraud and whoremongering, trade unions and bosses alike called for Berlusconi to resign.

The Merkozy duo vowed to deal with the crisis decisively in two summits in October (or rather four summits, given that each was split into an EU summit of 27 followed by a euro-zone meeting of 17). At the first gathering on October 23rd, Berlusconi was given an ultimatum to present credible reforms at the next meeting three days later. Asked at a press conference whether they were reassured by his response, Merkel and Sarkozy hesitated a bit too long, looked at each other and, as the room erupted in laughter, smiled and smirked. Involuntary, perhaps, but it was a humiliation for Berlusconi and a gesture of no confidence in Italy.

On October 26th the euro zone announced yet another "comprehensive solution". Italy promised to reform labour markets and pensions, cut red tape, abolish minimum charges for professional services and more. It would be subject to special monitoring by the Commission. And after another round of negotiations between leaders and banks, which barely seemed to involve the hapless Papandreou, Greek bonds would be subject to a 50% cut in face value (resulting in a 76% cut in terms of net present value). The aim was to bring Greece's debt down to 120% of GDP by 2020, a threshold chosen to match Italy's debt, which, by definition, had to be solvent.

To contain the impact, the euro zone needed bigger firewalls. Germany had been unwilling to increase its guarantees to the EFSF and many others were unable to do so, given the risk to their credit rating. France favoured giving the EFSF a banking licence, so that it could borrow from the ECB. But Trichet blocked the idea at a bad-tempered

FIG 5.1 **From crisis to crisis**
Ten-year bond yields, 2010–2012, %

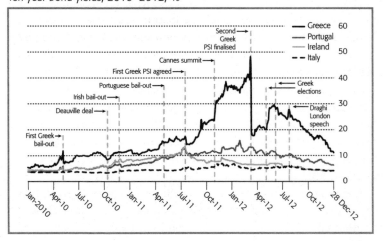

Source: Thomson Reuters

impromptu meeting on October 19th on the fringes of his official farewell celebration at Frankfurt's old opera house. So the summit set out two options. The EFSF could offer "credit enhancements" to insure investors against part of the loss on sovereign bonds; or it could create a special-purpose vehicle in which other countries willing to help Europe could invest. Leaders also agreed to bolster rickety banks by forcing them to find about €106 billion of extra capital by the end of June 2012 to meet a higher 9% threshold of "highest quality capital", after marking sovereign debt to market prices.

The deal was sealed with another layer of the favourite Franco-German mix: Sarkozy secured a commitment to hold twice-yearly euro-zone-only summits with the option, in future, of having a separate president; Merkel obtained support for yet another revision of the treaty aimed vaguely at "strengthening economic convergence within the euro area, improving fiscal discipline and deepening economic union". Yet within days the markets were struck by another bombshell: the Greek prime minister announced on October 31st that he would hold a referendum to approve the terms of the new rescue programme. Markets tumbled. The ECB worried that bank runs would start in Greece. After two years of crushing austerity, nobody could be expected to vote for more of it. Greek bond yields shot up, pulling everyone else along (see Figure 5.1). Italian bonds again pushed past the 6% mark. The euro zone was close to breaking.

Caned in Cannes

The system of peer-pressure, shy at first and then ever more insistent as the crisis worsened, reached its logical and brutal climax at the G20 summit hosted by Sarkozy in Cannes on November 3rd–4th 2011. Papandreou was summoned before Sarkozy, Merkel and leaders of European institutions on the eve of the summit. He was told he had shown himself "disloyal" after fellow leaders had worked hard to lift a large chunk of debt off Greece's shoulders. Until Greece approved the new programme, neither the euro zone nor the IMF would disburse a cent (*pas un sou*), said Sarkozy. And if Papandreou insisted on the referendum, the question should not be about the terms of the bail-out but about Greece's membership of the euro. If the cost of saving the euro was to let Greece go, so be it. Perhaps Greece could come back in after ten years, the French president suggested.

At a joint press conference by Sarkozy and Merkel the ultimatum was made public: "Does Greece want to remain in the euro zone, or not?" asked Sarkozy. For the first time in the crisis, the prospect of the euro breaking up was being openly discussed by its most important leaders. Papandreou vacillated. He left Cannes saying the question would indeed be about Greece's future in the euro, but once in Athens he declared it would be about the bail-out terms after all. Venizelos, who had been a brooding presence at the encounter in Cannes and was urged by some of those at the meeting to help stop the referendum, made his move: he declared his opposition to the ballot and led a revolt that precipitated Papandreou's downfall a week later.

On the morning of November 3rd, it was Berlusconi's turn to be roasted. Sarkozy and Wolfgang Schäuble, the German finance minister standing in for Merkel, demanded that Italy should apply for a precautionary line of credit from the IMF. Lagarde bluntly told the Italian prime minister that nobody believed him. With Zapatero in the room, the French president noted with disappointment that a

Spanish-style political solution – an early election in which the prime minister would not stand again – was not on offer in Italy. There was a touch of personal animosity: Sarkozy blamed Berlusconi personally for Italian newspapers' attacks on the French first lady, the Italian-born model and singer Carla Bruni.

For his part, Berlusconi seemed detached from the severity of his predicament and unprepared for the assault; "he was completely depressed," recounted one witness. Italy had always lived with high debt, Berlusconi told his peers; it could survive for a long time with higher interest rates and domestic savers could be counted on to buy bonds. He would refuse to take the IMF's line of credit – doing so would be tantamount to admitting that Italy had become another Greece, said his officials – but he would agree to intense monitoring by the Fund and the Commission. If Berlusconi was deflated inside the room, outside he tried to brazen his way out of isolation. "There is no crisis," he told journalists. "The restaurants are full and you cannot find a seat on the flights."

The Italian prime minister still enjoyed a degree of understanding from at least some in the room, including the placid Van Rompuy and the more irascible Barroso. Both thought a precautionary line of credit worth some €80 billion was far too small to help Italy's finances, and would only raise doubts about its solvency. That night Berlusconi also got unexpected support from Barack Obama, who normally had little time for Berlusconi but on this occasion sided with the doves. The American president all but took control of a side meeting of European leaders at the G20 summit. He urged the Europeans to act decisively, and concentrated his efforts on trying to convince Germany to enhance the European firewall. If the ECB persisted in refusing to intervene in an unlimited manner (for example, by issuing the EFSF a banking licence), how about contributing the Europeans' unused allocations of "special drawing rights"? SDRs are created by the IMF as a reserve asset, a sort of virtual gold, and their supply was greatly boosted in 2009 to give countries extra liquidity in the financial crisis. Now the tables were turned on Merkel. The idea was firmly blocked by the Bundesbank, which held Germany's allocation and regarded their use as tantamount to printing money. The German chancellor said she might relent if Italy accepted an IMF precautionary programme, but the idea did not fly. Merkel came under such concerted pressure, some of those in the room reported, that she was in tears, saying: "I was the hero, and now I am the villain."

Goodbye George and Silvio. And David too?

Within days of the Cannes summit, the pressure from Europe, markets and internal dissent had forced both George Papandreou and Silvio Berlusconi to resign, on November 8th and November 12th respectively. In their place came two technocratic prime ministers. Lucas Papademos, governor of the Greek central bank and a former vice-president of the ECB, was appointed in Athens. Mario Monti, a former European commissioner, was installed in Rome. Both were chosen, with a private nod from Brussels, for their close links to European policymakers. Their main task was to restore the credibility of their countries before their European peers and the faceless markets. Indeed, the arrival of the technocrats may have saved their countries from imminent economic disaster. But though they were called upon to clean up the mess created by the politicians, and endorsed in parliamentary votes, the manner of their appointment left a profound worry about democracy in Europe: as well as dictating economic policies, Europe was now, directly or indirectly, dictating the choice of political leaders.

Papademos and Monti could not, on their own, deal with a market crisis that was corroding the entire euro zone. Given the failure of the Cannes summit to bolster the firewall, the last line of defence was now the ECB. All eyes turned to the new man in Frankfurt, Mario Draghi. Appearing for the first time before the European Parliament on December 1st, he spoke opaquely about the advisability of a "fiscal compact", some kind of additional commitment to budgetary discipline. The effects of previous reforms and of the arrival of technocrats in Italy and Greece were not yet being felt, he explained. A compact enshrining new balanced-budget rules in a more formal framework would send an additional signal of credibility. He thus allied himself to Germany's cause for yet another treaty change.

The idea of a revision horrified just about everybody – even those outside the euro zone. For David Cameron, the British prime minister, the idea of a treaty revision was bound to stir his increasingly restive backbenchers to demand that he use the opportunity to win something for the UK. Cameron's diplomatic campaign was ill-prepared, particularly in his misreading of Merkel. His officials did not spell out the UK's demands – essentially the protection of the City of London from new EU financial regulation – until the eve of the December summit. The British had been lulled by EU legal experts into believing that the euro zone could not get around a UK veto. But when the crunch came in the small hours of December 9th, Cameron's attempt to veto the new fiscal compact treaty backfired. First, the EU's lawyers said the compact could, after all, be adopted as a separate agreement outside the EU's treaty. Second, most of the euro "outs" signed up to it, leaving the UK isolated. Back home Cameron was briefly hailed as a conquering hero, even though he had vetoed nothing at all. Sarkozy boasted privately that "we gave the British a slap in the face".

Desperate times

The brutality of the politics at the end of 2011 reflected the desperation of the moment. After nearly two years of errors and missed opportunities, the euro was close to breaking point. It was apparent that the Greek bail-out programme had been badly misjudged. The euro zone leaders tended to pin the blame on the impossible Greeks. If only they were more like the stoical Balts and just got on with controlling their deficit, said advocates of hard front-loaded austerity, they would have got over their pain more quickly. Latvia had suffered large losses of output, pegged its currency to the euro, suffered a banking bust and had to be bailed out by the IMF and European Commission. Yet Latvia rejected the IMF's advice to devalue the currency, and chose instead the agony of internal devaluation. It subsequently emerged as one of the fastest-growing countries in the EU. In the view of its leaders, the key ingredient was political will. Estonia underwent a similar experience. And as it joined the euro in 2011, Estonia intensely resented having to contribute to the bail-out of the far richer Greeks.

Internal devaluation is difficult at the best of times. The IMF's deputy managing director, Nemat Shafik, once memorably compared the process of recovering competitiveness to painting a house:

If you have an exchange rate, you can move your brush back and forth. If you don't have an exchange rate, you have to move the whole house.

Successful adjustment requires flexible labour markets and an open economy that can export its way back to growth, as well as a population willing to put up with the pain. Greece had none of these: it was a closed, rigid economy and its politics was polarised by a history of occupation, civil war and military rule. As such, Greece was the most recalcitrant of the euro-zone countries to be rescued. Greek leaders, even as they slashed the budget, did not understand how extensive structural reforms needed to be, and made no progress on privatisation. IMF experts returning from missions to Greece were increasingly alarmed by the dysfunctional public administration they found. And the Greek government was not helped by the opportunistic opposition that it had to contend with from the New Democracy party, which had, after all, run up the deficit in its last stint in government.

Even so, it was plain to all that Greece was being pushed into a recession that was far deeper than anyone had predicted. The situation was aggravated by successive statistical revisions that kept pushing back the country's starting point, and the crushing loss of investor confidence caused by the growing talk of Greece leaving the euro.

To many, the Deauville bargain is the grievous error that turned an admittedly risky Greek programme into a catastrophe. In reality, Deauville was only part of a wider confusion that gripped the Europeans from the start. They were in a muddle about whether Greece was solvent or bust, and thus vacillated over how to deal with its accumulated debt. They first chose a complete bail-out; then at Deauville suddenly flirted with the idea of across-the-board bail-in of creditors; and then backed away from the idea more or less entirely. By July, when they got around to cutting Greece's debt, the haircut was too modest and came too late. Months were wasted seeking a "voluntary" contribution from private creditors that would not trigger credit-default swaps (CDS); in the end CDS contracts were paid out anyway. The same uncertainty affected their judgment about the pace of fiscal consolidation. To make the numbers fit within the money made available by the euro zone and the IMF, Greece was forced into excessively harsh deficit-cutting (and at first had to pay high rates of interest). In contrast with Latvia, which cut its budget as its main trading partners were still stimulating their economies, Greece was trying to consolidate its budget while others were reducing deficits as well. Crucially, the Baltic states also had low debts to begin with; even after the worst of its recession, Latvia's debt stood at about 45% of GDP, less than half of Greece's at the start of its troubles.

A sober assessment in May 2010 should have judged that Greece's debt was unsustainable, and that it would have been better to cut the debt sooner rather than delay the inevitable. This would have resulted in a more realistic programme, focused less on austerity and more on structural reform, and better able to absorb the inevitable political and economic bumps. At the time, however, it might have been difficult to convince Germany that its banks had to take losses on Greek debt even as German taxpayers were being called upon to lend enormous sums to Greece. That said, even a large debt write-off would not have spared Greece a painful adjustment to close a budget deficit gap of 15% of GDP and a current-account deficit of similar magnitude.

Fudged assessments, unsustainable debt, inadequate financing, Greece's many political failures and uncertainty about the euro all fed the constant fear of a chaotic default. The Greek death spiral, and the incoherence of the euro zone's leaders, threatened to take down the whole currency. Contagion threatened to bring down Italy, the scariest debtor of all. Even with the will to act more decisively, governments would have struggled to find the money to stabilise the euro zone once Italy started to wobble. By the end of 2011, only the central bank had the resources to stabilise the system. What would it take for it to stand as the euro zone's lender of last resort?

6   Super Mario

A SPIKED PRUSSIAN MILITARY HELMET, a *Pickelhaube*, decorates Mario Draghi's office on the 35th floor of the Eurotower in Frankfurt, the headquarters of the ECB. It was a gift from the editors of *Bild*, a German tabloid newspaper, intended as both a compliment to his reputation as "the most German" of the candidates to run the central bank (after the resignation of Axel Weber) and a warning to the former Italian central banker not to let down his guard against inflation. As he took charge of the ECB at a time of great peril for the euro zone he had to act boldly, though he knew he could ill-afford to allow austere northerners to accuse him of turning the ECB, the heir to the uncompromising Bundesbank, into a European version of the Banca d'Italia.

Replacing Jean-Claude Trichet in November 2011, Draghi brought a new style. His meetings were shorter, he delegated much more responsibility to colleagues and, having spent time at Goldman Sachs, he was more in tune with markets than his predecessor, as well as rather less stuffy. His first act in November (and also in December) was to reverse his predecessor's misjudged rate rises earlier in the year, catching most analysts by surprise. It was a hint that, instead of being compelled to respond to events, he would try to change the market's expectations. The fiscal compact he had asked for also gave him political cover for a bolder move: the provision of vast amounts of emergency liquidity for Europe's banking system, called Long Term Refinancing Operations (LTRO). Banks and sovereigns were facing a large refinancing hump in 2012, and banks were running short of collateral. Draghi acted to prevent any funding "accidents" that might be the spark for another crisis.

The first wave of cash was announced just before the December 9th summit that endorsed the fiscal compact. The second wave was released in February 2012. In all, the ECB provided €1 trillion-worth of three-year loans at a 1% interest rate, and also eased collateral requirements. Nicolas Sarkozy gleefully let everybody know that the banks, especially in southern Europe, would use much of the money to buy high-yielding sovereign bonds; in other words, this was bond-buying through the back door of the banks. Yet the "Sarkozy trade", as it came to be known, did not save France from losing its AAA rating from Standard & Poor's (S&P) in January. Eight other euro-zone countries were also downgraded. By leaving Germany as its only AAA-rated euro-zone sovereign with a "stable" outlook, S&P destroyed the symbolic parity between Germany and France. Europe's dividing line shifted from the Alps and the Pyrenees to the Rhine. Moreover, by chastising so many, S&P made clear that the problem was not just individual countries, but the euro zone as a whole. The October summit deal had been inadequate and did not provide enough support for troubled states. It said:[1]

> The outcomes from the EU summit on Dec. 9, 2011, and subsequent statements from policymakers, lead us to believe that the agreement reached has not produced a breakthrough of sufficient size and scope to fully address the eurozone's financial problems ... We also believe that the agreement is predicated on only a partial recognition of the source of the crisis: that the current financial turmoil stems primarily from fiscal profligacy at the periphery of the eurozone. In our view, however, the financial problems facing the eurozone are as much a consequence of rising external imbalances and divergences in competitiveness between the eurozone's core and the so-called "periphery". As such, we believe that a reform process based on a pillar of fiscal austerity alone risks becoming self-defeating, as domestic demand falls in line with consumers' rising concerns about job security and disposable incomes, eroding national tax revenues.

Over the following weeks Draghi's cash would ease the spasm. The euro zone breathed more easily. Bond yields for Italy and Spain dropped markedly, by about 250 and 90 basis points respectively between January and March. The long-drawn-out second Greek bail-out, with its large haircut on privately held government bonds, was concluded in February and markets seemed unconcerned by the triggering of credit-default swaps that had once been so feared.

Draghi quietly retired Trichet's official bond-buying operation in February. Yet no sooner had he told *Bild* in March 2012 that "the worst is over" than the crisis entered another, more perilous phase. The LTRO drug was wearing off, and the euro zone had entered a double-dip recession at the end of 2011, caused in part by the previous year's turmoil. Markets' concern shifted from the deficit to shrinking output, that is, from the numerator to the denominator in the ratio of borrowing to GDP.

The pain in Spain

Through the crisis the spread of a country's bond yields over German ones has been the temperature chart of the euro zone's sickness. The spread in bond yields between Italy and Spain tells its own story of comparative illness. Before the credit crunch, Italian bonds would yield 10–20 basis points more than Spanish ones. In January 2010 the lines flipped, in part because conservative Italian banks seemed in better shape than Spanish ones, crippled as they were by the property crash. In August 2011, though, Italy was again the riskier bet as Silvio Berlusconi's government began to collapse. In March 2012, the order was inverted once more (see Figure 6.2 on page 89).

There were two main reasons for the latest switch. First, Italy's Mario Monti became the darling of Europe, feted in Germany and the United States alike. Monti, some officials said, was Italy's real firewall. In Spain, meanwhile, doubts spread about the credibility of the new conservative government of Mariano Rajoy, even though it had been resoundingly elected in November 2011 on a promise of tough deficit-cutting and structural reforms. Second, Spain's economy and its banks were taking a turn for the worse.

In late February Spain announced it would miss its 2011 deficit target by a surprisingly wide margin, 8.5% of GDP instead of 6%. On March 2nd Rajoy unilaterally changed the 2012 target to 5.8%, instead of the EU-mandated 4.4%. That he made the announcement on the margins of an EU summit at which 25 leaders signed the fiscal compact recommitting governments to budget discipline, informing nobody of his move, caused much irritation; a feeling heightened by the fact that he withheld publication of his 2012 budget until after a regional election in Andalusia to be held at the end of the month (his party lost anyway).

Spain's woes caused a deeper rethink among European policymakers. Spain gave strong cause to question the diagnosis of the euro's problems. This was not a case of profligacy, as in Greece, or reckless "Anglo-Saxon" capitalism, as in Ireland. Spain had run a budget surplus before the crisis and had boasted of having one of the best financial regulatory systems. Moreover, Spain's persistent budget deficit raised questions about the favoured prescription of hard, front-loaded austerity. In April the IMF published the first of a series of studies suggesting that fiscal multipliers, which measure how badly growth would be affected by budget austerity, were larger than expected in circumstances, such as those of the euro zone, in which interest rates were close to zero, credit was tight and neighbouring countries were all cutting their deficits. The Fund urged euro-zone countries to slow the pace of fiscal consolidation.

Above all, the alarming state of Spain's banks highlighted a facet of the crisis that had been semi-neglected: the banking crisis of 2009, masked by the panic over sovereign debt, had not been resolved. In fact the two were interconnected. In Greece the bankrupt sovereign was bringing down the banks. In Ireland, and increasingly now Spain, bust banks were endangering the sovereign. The outflow of capital that Spain had suffered from the summer of 2011 abruptly accelerated pace in March 2012.

Spain's financial regulator had proved unable or unwilling to clean up banks wrecked by bad property loans. Across the euro zone, and beyond, banking was one of the last bastions of protection within the EU. Regulators treated banks as national champions. They were reluctant to reveal losses, either for lack of money to recapitalise banks, or for fear that they would be taken over by foreigners. Often governments wanted to avoid rescued banks being forced to divest themselves of assets under state-aid rules designed to preserve fair competition. By mid-2012, say EU officials, national regulators had overestimated bank assets in almost all cases the Commission had

FIG 6.1 **The deadly embrace**
Spain: five-year CDS premiums on sovereign and bank debt, 2007–12

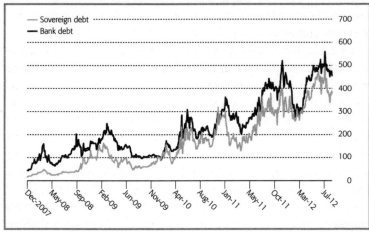

Sources: Thomson Reuters; Silvia Merler and Jean Pisani-Ferry, Bruegel

investigated, probably in an attempt to mask the scale of public assistance. Repeated stress tests conducted by the European Banking Authority had been discredited: in July 2011 it gave a clean bill of health to Dexia, a French-Belgian group that was bailed out in October 2011, and to Spain's Bankia, part-nationalised in May 2012. The LTRO money had provided brief relief, but by encouraging banks to buy more bonds had worsened the deadly feedback loop.

In sum, Spain provided strong evidence that the problem was not just the behaviour of individual countries, or the enforcement of fiscal rules. Instead, it was property bubbles, imbalances and the unstable structure of the euro zone. Indeed, the euro zone found itself in the grip of three separate crises – banking, sovereign debt and growth – with each connected to the other through destabilising feedback loops. Figure 6.1 shows how premiums for credit-default swaps for Spanish sovereign bonds and Spanish banks closely followed each other. Weak banks endangered sovereigns that were called upon to save them, and weak sovereigns endangered banks holding bonds at risk of default. Recession worsened the debt ratio, but austerity to reduce borrowing suppressed growth, or caused even worse recession.

Federal governments attenuate such doom-loops by providing fiscal transfers (for example, through unemployment benefits) and dealing with shocks to the financial system. But the euro zone had no budget or central authority.

One response was gradually to ease austerity. Already the second Greek programme in February had relaxed the pace of fiscal consolidation and softened repayment terms on bail-out loans. In late May, despite the irritation with Rajoy's antics, the Commission gave Spain an extra year to meet its deficit target of 3% of GDP by 2014, instead of 2013. In June it was given a partial bail-out when finance ministers agreed in principle to lend it up to €100 billion to help clean up and recapitalise its banks. Unlike Greece, Spain was given only "light" conditions, and the sum included a generous safety margin to address unforeseen needs. But the deal had little impact on borrowing costs. And now Spain's troubles were once again pushing up Italy's bond yields.

Europe à l'Hollandaise

The election on May 6th 2012 of a Socialist president in France, François Hollande, who had campaigned on an anti-austerity platform, was greeted with mixed feelings: hope that the Merkozy diktat would end, but also worry that the untested Merkhollande might lead to paralysis or worse. There was not much of a honeymoon. On the same day, Greek voters crushed both main centrist parties, the centre-right New Democracy and especially the Socialist Pasok. The old giants barely mustered 30% of the vote between them. It was, in a sense, as if the abortive referendum that cost George Papandreou his job had been held after all. But having expressed their revulsion with the political elite, Greek voters were less clear about what should replace it. Votes were scattered among anti-austerity factions ranging from the Stalinist left to the neo-Nazi right. A second ballot was called in June to break the stalemate, amid hopes that the Greeks would behave rather like the French: voting with their hearts in the first round but with their heads in the second.

Hollande soon cast himself as the champion of the south. His promise to renegotiate the fiscal compact was fobbed off with a "growth compact" that was little more than a repackaging of several modest and pre-existing European spending initiatives. He also revived the idea of Eurobonds. It was unfair that Spain had to borrow at 6% while Germany could do so almost free of interest, said Hollande at an informal EU summit to welcome him on May 23rd. But Angela Merkel would not hear of debt mutualisation. That evening Herman Van Rompuy appointed himself to write a report with a vague remit to find ways of deepening euro-zone integration. It would look not only at Eurobonds but also, crucially, at "more integrated banking supervision and resolution, and a common deposit-insurance scheme".

The idea of a "banking union", as an alternative to the "fiscal union" pushed by France, was thus taking shape as a response to the Spanish crisis. Economists had long argued that, in an integrated financial market, centralised European authorities should be responsible for supervising banks and for winding them up when they failed. In February 2011 a paper by Bruegel, a Brussels think-tank, declared that "nothing less than supranational banking supervision and resolution bodies can handle the kind of financial interdependence that now exists in Europe". Such ideas had been considered for Jacques de Larosière's report on financial regulation in February 2009, but were deemed too ambitious. The new European supervisory authorities – three new regulators for banks, insurance and markets, and the European Systemic Risk Board to monitor threats to the overall financial system – that emerged from the report were little more than loose co-ordinating bodies.

A separate but related idea was the direct recapitalisation of troubled banks by the EFSF or the future ESM, to avoid the burden falling on vulnerable sovereigns. The concept had been pushed by the IMF in July 2011. France had also wanted to draw on the EFSF to recapitalise Dexia in October 2011 but had been turned down. In April 2012 the IMF returned to the charge, this time with a more detailed longer-term proposal for a single European supervisor with a single resolution authority and fund, and a Europe-wide deposit-guarantee scheme. By the end of May the chorus of supporters for "banking union" grew louder, as the ECB and the Commission joined in. Under the deliberately understated title of "integrated financial framework", banking union was one of the four pillars of Van Rompuy's June 26th report on the future of the euro, alongside fiscal union (including tighter budget controls and a timetable for Eurobonds), economic union (co-ordination of labour-market and other policies) and political union (to give democratic legitimacy and accountability to the other three pillars).[2]

The breakthrough came at a secret meeting of finance ministers from Germany, France, Italy and Spain and senior European officials, at the Sheraton Hotel next to Charles de Gaulle airport in Paris (for greater discretion) on June 26th. The discussion focused on another old French demand, that the firewall be boosted by giving the ESM a banking licence so it could borrow from the ECB. Changing tack, Pierre Moscovici, the new French finance minister, suggested direct bank recapitalisation by the ESM to help Spain. His German counterpart, Wolfgang Schäuble, caused a stir when he suggested it might be possible – but only if there were direct supervision of banks. This was in line with Germany's mantra: greater solidarity could only come with greater control. But would Merkel agree to any of this?

Two Super Marios

The European football championship, in which Italy met Germany in the semi-final at the national stadium in Warsaw on June 28th 2012, became a metaphor for the political battle taking place the same night in Brussels: north and south, discipline against guile, creditors versus debtors. The football-mad Merkel would step out of the meeting room to watch replays of key moments, such as Mario Balotelli's winning goal for Italy in the 36th minute. In the summit she was confronted by another Super Mario, the Italian prime minister, Mario Monti. His game was a form of *catenaccio*, the unyielding Italian defence, played with his Spanish colleague. They stubbornly blocked agreement on the final communiqué, including Hollande's "growth pact", until the chancellor had agreed to their demands. Rajoy wanted the direct recapitalisation of Spanish banks by the EFSF; Monti wanted an automatic mechanism to help bring down the borrowing costs of vulnerable but "virtuous" countries (that is, Italy).

For Italy, in particular, this was an unusual change of behaviour.

Berlusconi, though dominant for years in domestic politics, typically said very little at European summits. Now the technocrat who had succeeded him was daring to play hardball against the mighty Germans. The difference, perhaps, was down to the fact that Italy under Monti had regained some credibility, and therefore some room for manoeuvre. With some skilful bureaucratic midfield play by senior officials in Brussels, Monti and Rajoy got their way at around 4am, having overcome a sustained rearguard action by Finland and the Netherlands (one senior euro-zone official called these last two *emmerdeurs*, a fruity French word that translates roughly as "pains in the arse".)

Thus the opening sentence of the euro-zone statement declared grandly: "We affirm that it is imperative to break the vicious circle between banks and sovereigns."[3] Leaders agreed to set up a single supervisor, based at the ECB, to oversee the euro zone's 6,000-odd banks. Thereafter, the rescue funds could be used to recapitalise troubled banks directly. Ireland was also promised unspecified help, in tacit recognition that it had been forced to take on much of its banks' debts. The second concession was to allow the EFSF, and in future the ESM, to intervene to stabilise bond markets for members respecting a long list of European commitments without a full-blown troika-monitored programme.

Rajoy probably scored the winning goal on the night, but Monti was the playmaker. He certainly acted as the victor, as he emerged from the summit speaking teasingly about "many important discussions, sometimes tense, with many emotional aspects, often concentrated on football"; his supporters would later say that an oblique reference in the communique to the ECB's role as an "agent" for bond-buying by the rescue funds was the harbinger of a bigger role for the ECB. Across Europe, newspapers could not resist parallels between Germany's defeat in European football and Merkel's concession in European politics. Pro-Berlusconi papers, no fans of Monti, were particularly crude. One showed Balotelli kicking a football in the shape of Merkel's head; another splashed with the headline "*Ciao, Ciao Culona*" ("Bye Bye Fat Arse"), a reference to an intercepted phone call in which Berlusconi is alleged have described the German chancellor in particularly crude terms.[4]

The euro zone was crossing an important threshold: responsibility for the banks might now be shared. Some EU officials spoke of the summit as the most important act of integration since the Maastricht treaty. Of itself, the creation of a single supervisor would amount to a substantial surrender of national sovereignty. The change would be greater still if and when other pillars of banking union were created: a euro-zone resolution authority with access to a common pot of money to wind up bust banks; a single deposit-guarantee scheme; and a common fiscal backstop. The US Federal Deposit Insurance Corporation (FDIC) is set up along such lines, able to draw on a line of credit from the Treasury if necessary. From the start of the financial crisis to the end of 2013, it has wound up more than 400 (mostly small) banks, in contrast with a handful in Europe (and about 40 banks that have received state aid). Merkel may have told members of her coalition that she could not envisage wholesale Eurobonds in her lifetime. But joint liability of a different form might now come via the back door of the banks. In the end, the need for taxpayers ultimately to stand behind the banking system means that a real banking union would become a step towards a fiscal union.

Still not enough

Yet the euphoria in the markets was short-lived. Part of the blame lies with European leaders' love of bickering. The Dutch prime minister, Mark Rutte, tried to peg back Monti's exuberance, insisting countries would still face conditions if helped by the fund. Finland demanded collateral, and later seemed to muse about leaving the euro (officials said comments to this effect by Jutta Urpilainen, the finance minister, had been mistranslated). Germany put out the message that, even in the case of direct recapitalisation, national governments would be liable for any banking losses. And there was another worry. Germany's constitutional court was due to deliver its verdict on the legality of the permanent new rescue fund, the European Stability Mechanism, in September. A negative decision would remove the euro zone's safety net, inadequate as it may have been. More bad news came from Moody's, a ratings agency, which announced it had placed the AAA credit rating of Germany, the Netherlands and

Luxembourg on "negative outlook" because of the danger of financial instability if Greece left the euro, and the possible costs of helping Spain and Italy.[5]

On top of this was the chronic, seemingly insoluble problem of Greece. Despite two bail-outs, two rounds of debt restructuring and, as in Italy, the appointment of a technocrat to head the government, Greece needed still more billions to avoid default. All attempts at reform had come to a halt during the Greek election campaign. The second ballot on June 17th allowed Antonis Samaras, leader of New Democracy, to cobble together a broad coalition with his arch-rival, Pasok. Yet Samaras was poorly regarded by European leaders. In opposition his refusal to support the first bail-out was deemed to have crippled Papandreou. Later, when he backed the unity government of Lucas Papademos, Samaras was evasive about the terms of the second rescue. And by forcing early elections in the midst of a wrenching adjustment, he was blamed for opening the door to extremists.

For better or worse, Samaras was now the last hope for Greece. Barroso flew to Athens to warn him to stop talking about renegotiating Greece's bail-out conditions. In private and in public, he told him: "Deliver, deliver, deliver." To the outrage of many in Brussels, Merkel's government continued to entertain the idea of pushing Greece out, even though its citizens had voted for pro-European parties. Philipp Rösler, leader of Germany's liberal Free Democrats, Merkel's junior coalition partner, declared on July 22nd: "A withdrawal of Greece has long since lost its terror." By then Spanish ten-year bond yields had passed the psychological threshold of 7%, and Italian ones were not far behind. Terror had returned to the euro zone.

Whatever it takes

To some, Cannes and its aftermath in late 2011 was the cruellest moment of the entire crisis. To many others, the moment of greatest despair came in the summer of 2012. Draghi, spending a few days in London at the end of July, was worried about financial data: economic fundamentals had not changed and there was ample liquidity. Yet money was fleeing north, regulators were telling banks to keep their money within national borders, cross-border bank lending had all but stopped, and sovereign spreads were rising along with credit-default swaps. To the ECB this was evidence of the euro zone moving towards the "bad equilibrium" evoked by Paul De Grauwe, then a professor of economics at the Catholic University of Leuven. He had argued in 2011 that, unless the ECB acted as a lender of last resort, countries in the euro zone were effectively borrowing in a foreign currency and could easily be pushed into default by panicked markets. Draghi thought that fear of the euro's break-up was becoming a self-fulfilling process. Only the ECB could put an end to the "redenomination risk".

On July 26th, the eve of the summer's other big sporting festival, the London Olympics, Draghi addressed a group of investors gathered in the splendour of Lancaster House in London. The single currency, he recalled,[6] had once been described as a bumblebee which, as scientific lore had it, should not be able to fly. The euro area was "much, much stronger than people acknowledge today"; outsiders were underestimating recent reforms and the political will to make the euro irreversible. Then came a seemingly unscripted sentence that made his audience sit up. "Within our mandate, the ECB is ready to do whatever it takes to preserve the euro," said Draghi, pausing for a moment. "And believe me, it will be enough." Dealing with markets' fear of "convertibility risk", declared Draghi, was within the remit of the ECB.

Markets had usually ignored leaders' promises to do whatever it took to save the currency. But Draghi's words had an immediate effect, even though nobody was quite sure what would follow – not even all members of the ECB's executive board. There could not simply be a return to Trichet's Securities Market Programme (SMP), by now regarded as an expensive mistake that had lumbered the ECB with more than €200 billion-worth of vulnerable bonds, to little effect. Draghi never forgot how Berlusconi had reneged on his promises of reform the previous year. The ECB concluded that the SMP had suffered from multiple flaws. It had no means of compelling countries to reform. It was limited in scope, so never amounted to the "big bazooka" needed to ward off speculators. Its resources were scattered across a range of maturities. And it left the ECB exposed politically.

So now Draghi reinvented the formula. His new policy of outright monetary transactions (OMT), outlined on August 4th and then set out in detail on September 6th, would require countries seeking ECB intervention to request help from the rescue fund and sign up to a macroeconomic adjustment programme. The fund would have to intervene in the primary bond market. Only then would the ECB decide whether to intervene in the secondary market, where it would concentrate on buying short-dated bonds with a maturity of less than three years. Crucially, there would be no pre-set limit to the quantities it could buy. In other words, it would be left to governments to decide whether a country was solvent, and overtly to impose reforms, rather than leaving the ECB to send out secret letters. And the ECB would concentrate its potentially huge firepower on a narrow front of the bond market.

Even so, OMT was resisted by the Bundesbank's president, Jens Weidmann, who voted against the policy, saying it was akin to printing money. But unlike his predecessor, Axel Weber, he did not resign. Tellingly, his colleagues from Finland and the Netherlands – the traditional *emmerdeurs* – voted in favour. And the German government made clear its support for Draghi. Weidmann sounded increasingly like a prophet in the wilderness, declaring that saving the euro was a job for elected leaders, not central bankers. At one point he couched his criticism in literary terms, by quoting Goethe's *Faust*: in the play the Holy Roman Emperor complains of being short of gold; Mephistopheles persuades him to sign a document which is then reproduced and distributed as paper money; but after the initial economic upswing comes inevitable inflation and collapse.[7] The lesson, said Weidmann, was that central banks must avoid the temptation of solving short-term problems by creating money lest they create long-term damage. To which the ECB's insiders retorted: the Bundesbank always has a solution for the long term, never for the short term.

The impact of OMT exceeded all expectations. From the end of July onwards, bond yields of the most troubled states came down almost continuously. By the end of 2012 Italian and Spanish bond yields had fallen to about 5% each (the spread over German bonds was still 200 basis points). More good news came in September, when Germany's constitutional court gave the go-ahead for the ratification of the ESM, the permanent rescue fund, subject to minor caveats. The fund came into existence in early October. Based on paid-in capital rather than guarantees, the ESM was a more robust instrument than the EFSF it was replacing (the two will overlap for some years).

Draghi would later tell senior euro-zone policymakers that the commitment to start a banking union had created the conditions for OMT. As another ECB insider put it:

> We were willing to build a bridge, but it could not be a bridge to nowhere. The leaders had to build a road on the other side.

At the time of writing, markets had not called Draghi's bluff. OMT, according to one ECB insider, was "by far the most significant intervention of monetary history." It had not cost a cent, and did not stoke inflation. Even Weidmann would admit, in private, that it had worked better than he would have expected.

No Grexit

Even with the ECB's intervention, the future of the euro zone could not be settled until the question of Greece was resolved. What to do? Merkel had never been among those most militantly pushing for the expulsion of Greece; she had even described herself in private conversations as the only person in Germany still willing to keep the Greeks in. As she told the Bundestag in February 2012, "I should and have to take risks, but I cannot embark on adventures." She had allowed her ministers to use the threat of expulsion to exert pressure on Greece to abide by its programme and, latterly, to convince voters to support pro-European parties.

Throughout the crisis, Merkel had received contradictory advice, both at home and abroad. Some at the IMF thought Greece would be better off returning to the drachma given the euro zone's muddled policies. At the same time, José Manuel Barroso, president of the European Commission, warned Merkel that Grexit might cause so much political instability as to provoke another military intervention. But during August 2012 Merkel made a firm decision: Greece would stay in the euro, even if that took more money. Some think the moment of clarity came during her walking holiday in the Italian Alps, or soon after her return to Berlin. Others suggest the final decision was taken during a trip to China at the end of the month, when she was grilled by Chinese leaders about the future of the euro zone. What made up her mind were her conversations with Weidmann and the ECB's Jörg Asmussen. Neither could offer any assurance that the consequences of Grexit could be contained.

When the newly elected Samaras, recovering from eye surgery, visited Berlin on August 24th, Merkel already sounded much more sympathetic to the plight of Greece. She told him privately she was ready to "help" if Greece wanted to leave the euro; but if it wanted to stay, she needed assurances that Samaras would deliver reform and fiscal discipline. The Greek prime minister said Grexit was inconceivable, and he would resign immediately if it were ever on the cards.

The strongest signal that Greece would stay came on October 9th, when Merkel made her first trip to Greece, expressed her desire that the country should stay in and offered "practical" assistance with structural reforms, such as German experts to help overhaul tax administration and modernise local government. Her attempt to empathise with the Greeks was not universally welcomed. Protesters outside parliament waved banners declaring "Angela you are not welcome". Municipal workers in full Nazi uniform, one of them with a Hitler moustache, drove a jeep flying swastika flags through the streets as a reminder of the German occupation in the second world war. Riot police resorted to tear gas and stun grenades to keep protesters from the parliament building.

Although Germany no longer wanted to throw Greece out, it still did not want to lend it more billions to keep it in. A third programme would not go down well in the Bundestag. So Greece had to find large savings (worth more than 7% of GDP) in 2013 and 2014 to make up for the time lost earlier in the year and to deal with the consequences of a deeper-than-expected recession. It would be given two more years to reach its target of a primary budget surplus of 4.5% of GDP in 2016 instead of 2014. That would require more loans in future, and more loans would raise the debt. For now the most contentious issue was the tug-of-war between the IMF and the euro zone over the size of Greece's debt. Greece's economic outlook was so poor that it would probably miss by a long shot the target of bringing debt down to 120% of GDP by 2020. The figure was now expected to be 144% of GDP. The IMF sought outright forgiveness of debt, now mostly held by the official lenders (hence the term official sector involvement, or OSI). It said a write-off would be the strongest possible signal of the euro zone's intent to keep Greece in, and so would boost investor confidence. Yet OSI was unacceptable ahead of Germany's general election in September 2013; it would have vindicated critics who said money lent to Greece would never be repaid.

After much wrangling, a deal in November again cut Greece's interest rate, deferred payment for ten years and doubled maturities to 30 years. It included a commitment to cut Greece's debt to 124% of GDP in 2020 and to "substantially below" 110% of GDP two years later, with the promise to take more action if necessary once Greece reached a primary budget surplus. Nevertheless, an important line had been crossed. Without saying so too loudly, the euro zone was ready to pay to keep Greece in the currency. Spain and Italy were already lending to Greece at a lower rate than they could borrow.

Banking disunion

The largest cloud over the unaccustomed optimism in the autumn of 2012 was Germany's backtracking on banking union. The Commission rushed out its legislative proposals for a single bank supervisor in September but Germany made sure that key parts of the document, such as a timetable for the creation of a common deposit-insurance system, were excised. There was only a vague commitment to creating a bank-resolution authority for the euro zone to complement the supervisor. The immediate focus would be on harmonising national banking rules across the EU as a whole, including "bail-in" procedures to impose losses on shareholders, bondholders and large depositors in order to spare the taxpayer.

Even the supervisor was not entirely to Germany's liking. The Commission wanted the ECB-based supervisor to oversee all 6,000-plus banks in the euro zone. Germany insisted it should focus only on the bigger "systemic" banks, leaving supervision of smaller banks, including its own often-troubled *Sparkassen* and *Landesbanken*, in national hands – even though Spain's experience showed that trouble in small lenders could become systemic. Germany also slowed down the timetable for the supervisor to start work (originally January 1st 2013) on the grounds that such an important task should not be rushed. Thereafter, direct bank recapitalisation should only take place once the system had shown itself to be "effective".

Worse was to come. On September 25th Wolfgang Schäuble, the German finance minister, and his Dutch and Finnish colleagues sought to limit the commitment to direct recapitalisation: it should apply only to new problems, not "legacy assets", and should only be a "last resort", after using private capital and then national funds. Spain gave up on the idea of direct recapitalisation of its banks. In December it borrowed €41 billion of the €100 billion allocated by the euro zone, which would increase its debt ratio by about 4% of GDP. Ireland's hope that its bank debt would be taken over retroactively was similarly dashed.

At the end of 2012 finance ministers reached a compromise on the scope of the new supervisor: it would directly oversee the biggest "systemic" banks in the euro zone (about 130), while day-to-day control of smaller lenders would be left to national regulators, subject to central rules and the right of the euro-zone supervisor to assume oversight of any bank if deemed necessary. Beyond banking union, the other pillars of Van Rompuy's "genuine" economic and monetary union were also crumbling. In October he had dropped the idea of a timetable for Eurobonds. At a summit in December he tried to push the concept of "fiscal capacity", a French-sponsored idea to create a central budget to act as a counter-cyclical economic tool to stabilise countries undergoing a downturn, maybe by providing benefits for short-term unemployment. But this was killed too.

What remained of Van Rompuy's roadmap was only a timetable for the next step on banking union – the creation of a bank-resolution mechanism – along with the wisp of a German idea to have "contracts" between governments and the Commission to promote structural reforms. In a nod to France, these could include some extra money. This was less ambitious than early German ideas to establish some kind of system of transfers to help the most troubled countries. It was certainly not the French idea of an automatic stabiliser. The Commission published its own "blueprint" for reform in November to try to keep some of these ideas alive, but EU leaders had lost interest in making great federalist leaps, if they ever harboured the notion in the first place. Ahead of the German election due in September 2013, Merkel was wary of taking on new liabilities. She had already lost her "chancellor's majority" in votes to approve bail-out programmes, meaning that she now had to rely on votes from the opposition Social Democrats.

In some ways Draghi's threat of unlimited intervention worked too well. As pressure from markets eased, so did the pressure to fix the euro zone. The danger of moral hazard did not apply just to debtors; it applied to creditor countries too. Leaders may have pledged to do "whatever it takes", but more often it was a matter of doing "as little as we can get away with".

Ugliness on Aphrodite's island

The new doctrines of banking union would be tested sooner than expected, in the case of Cyprus. The Commission's proposed rules on "bail-in" were pencilled in to apply from 2018. Germany wanted them in 2015. But in Cyprus bail-in would be applied immediately, and in the most chaotic manner possible.

The easternmost country in the European Union, closer to Syria than to Belgium, France or Germany, Cyprus has always been an awkward member. It entered the EU in 2004 as a divided island, voters in the Greek-Cypriot republic having rejected a UN plan to reunite with the Turkish-Cypriot north (where the plan was supported) on the eve of its accession to the EU. The Greek-Cypriot government used and abused EU institutions to wage its feud with its northern rival and Turkey, and to lend support to Russia. With an oversized financial sector (more than eight times GDP), catering mostly for Russian expatriates, Cyprus was vulnerable when the financial crisis struck in 2008. It was shut out of markets in May 2011 and then suffered a double blow: its banks took large losses as a result of their exposure to Greece (including losses equivalent to 25% of GDP as a result of the haircut on Greek bonds); and the main power station, generating about half of Cyprus's electricity, was destroyed by the explosion of a cache of weapons stored carelessly nearby.

Cyprus's pre-crisis boom was clearly unsustainable. A long-running current-account deficit gaped ever wider. Companies and households were hugely in debt. And government debt, though comparatively low, was rising because of overgenerous civil-service pay and benefits (including index-linked pay rises twice a year). With a short-term loan from Russia running out, and a ratings downgrade that meant Cypriot debt was no longer eligible as collateral at the ECB, Cyprus belatedly turned to the EU for help in June 2012, just as it took over the rotating EU presidency. Negotiations progressed slowly. Ahead of the presidential election in January 2013, the communist incumbent, Demetris Christofias, said he would not stand again. But he refused to entertain the fiscal cuts the troika would demand; and he was firmly opposed to any privatisation. The euro zone was in no rush: it had enough on its plate with Greece and Spain, and nobody was keen to bail out banks stuffed with Russian money, some of which might have been the fruit of corrupt dealings. Better to wait until after the election, many felt.

Merkel had been among leaders of the conservative European People's Party who went to Cyprus to support Nicos Anastasiades, leader of the centre-right DISY party, a month before he comfortably won the presidential election in February 2013. But his political "family" was less than generous when it came to negotiating a bail-out. The IMF, now less malleable as a result of the fiasco in Greece, said lending Cyprus the €17 billion needed to recapitalise its banks and finance public spending would make its debt unsustainable. Greek-style haircuts on government bonds were unappealing, because much of the debt was held by Cypriot banks. Moreover, the euro zone had vowed that the Greek PSI would be an exception. The expected bounty of natural gas off Cyprus's coast was too uncertain, and the prospect of commercial exploitation too tangled in regional geopolitics. So a large share of the money would have to come from the two big banks: Bank of Cyprus and Cyprus Popular Bank, known as Laiki.

On March 16th Anastasiades stayed in Brussels at the end of an EU summit to be on hand for bail-out negotiations. The talks turned ugly when he rejected any large-scale hit on depositors, the ECB threatened to cut off liquidity to the large Cypriot banks, and Anastasiades threatened to leave the euro. A compromise was found, but it was a bad one. All depositors would be subject to a one-off "levy": 9.9% on large deposits and 6.75% on those below the €100,000 deposit-guarantee limit. Somehow the euro zone, working late at night and run by a novice (Jeroen Dijsselbloem, the Dutch finance minister, had recently become chairman of the Eurogroup), agreed to raid the savings of grandmothers rather than impose a bigger haircut on Russian oligarchs. The mess came down to a fetish about round numbers. Germany said the euro zone would lend no more than €10 billion; the IMF insisted the island's debt should be kept below 100% of GDP by 2020 (a more exacting standard than for Greece, on the grounds that it was a small economy); and Anastasiades was adamant that any tax on big depositors should be below 10%.

As banks were shut in Cyprus to avoid an outrush of money, there followed a week of brinkmanship, including a 36–0 vote in the Cypriot parliament to reject the terms, street protests, a failed attempt by Cyprus to throw itself at Russia's feet and a public ultimatum by the ECB. Van Rompuy stepped in to try to fix the mess. On March 24th Anastasiades was flown back to Brussels on a Belgian air force plane. He resisted the IMF's attempt to wind up both Bank of Cyprus and Laiki. That would crush the island's economy, he said. In the end he agreed to sacrifice Laiki to save a rump of Bank of Cyprus. Laiki's bad assets and all its uninsured deposits were put into a "bad bank". Its viable assets and insured deposits were put into a "good bank" and transferred to Bank of Cyprus (along with, questionably, Laiki's obligation to repay the ECB's liquidity loans). Bank of Cyprus would be restructured by wiping out shareholders. Junior and senior bondholders were bailed in and given equity. Uninsured depositors were subjected to haircuts of 47.5%, also in exchange for equity. The remaining deposits were for the most part put into term deposit accounts for up to two years.

The new deal was better than the old one, in that it protected insured depositors and concentrated the pain on the two largest banks, which had been the cause of the problem. It restored a sensible hierarchy of creditors in bank resolution, whereas under the previous agreement, senior bondholders would have been spared but small depositors hit. But it came at a cost. The Cypriot economy was pushed into a deep slump, albeit perhaps not as catastrophic as some feared.

The euro zone for the first time introduced capital controls, meaning that a euro in Cyprus no longer carried the same value as a euro elsewhere. The reputation of the euro zone in managing the crisis was further tarnished. And the judgment of the ECB, now charged with supervising the biggest banks, was also questioned. It had provided liquidity to Laiki, even though it was bust, and then insisted on being repaid fully when the bank was wound up. Moreover, it had been party to the original deal that undermined the EU-wide €100,000 guarantee to depositors.

Had Cyprus walked out of the euro, as some expected, European officials were ready with a proposals for a blanket guarantee on all deposits in the euro zone and the activation of OMT. Such ideas were dismissed by the Germans. The proposition was never tested, as Anastasiades caved in. Tellingly, sovereign- and corporate-bond markets were sanguine throughout the week-long standoff. Draghi's firewall held firm. Plainly, Cyprexit in 2013 did not hold the same terror as Grexit had in 2011 or 2012.

Good news, at last

Little seemed to scare the euro zone any more. The possibility of a bail-out for Slovenia, which was grappling with the collapse of its opaque banking system, part of a web of political patronage, was treated as a tidying-up exercise. Through 2013 bond yields in peripheral countries declined gradually but steadily, perturbed only on occasion. Spreads over German bonds, which had exceeded 600 basis points for Spain and 500 for Italy in July 2012, fell steadily to below 200 basis points for both by February 2014. Their bond yields fell to pre-crisis levels (see Figure 6.2). Even Greece, whose spread peaked at 2,900 basis points in June 2012, was down to about 650. And, haltingly at first, economic growth returned to the euro zone. No country had left the euro, and several still wanted to join. Latvia, the poster-child for hard, front-loaded austerity with a fixed currency (its currency was pegged to the euro) joined on January 1st 2014, following Estonia, which entered in 2011. Lithuania wants to be next.

Current-account deficits in the periphery narrowed, not just because imports collapsed but also because exports were rising. With the easing of the financial crisis, the pace of austerity was sensibly

FIG 6.2 **Safe landing**
Ten-year government-bond yields, July 2011–December 2013, %

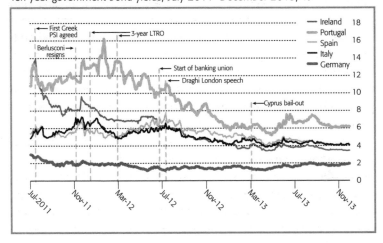

Source: Thompson Reuters

relaxed. In May 2013 France, Spain and Slovenia were given an extra two years to meet their deficit target of 3% of GDP. The Netherlands and Portugal got an extra year. Italy came out of its excessive deficit procedure in June. That said, tougher fiscal rules known as the "two-pack" came into force in the autumn of 2013, obliging countries to submit their draft budgets for 2014 to the Commission for comment before being sent to national parliaments. Increasingly, the Commission focused its yearly policy recommendations on promoting structural reforms, though even that was resented by France, with Hollande telling Brussels not to "dictate" specific reforms. To the irritation of Merkel's government, the Commission plucked up the courage in November to launch an in-depth study of Germany's large and persistent current-account surplus.

Both Ireland and Spain opted for a "clean" end to their bail-out programmes at the end of 2013. The move may yet prove to be hubristic. IMF programmes usually end with a line of credit to facilitate a full return to market financing. Ireland and Spain may not have had much choice in the matter. Merkel was not keen to ask the Bundestag for more money. It suited her to have the strongest possible demonstration of the success of the policies she had enacted (and often changed). And it suited her Irish and Spanish counterparts to boast that they were free of the dreaded troika. But their emancipation may result in prolonged servitude for Portugal. Despite its compliance with bail-out conditions, Portugal suffered a wobble in the spring of 2013 when its constitutional court blocked some deficit-cutting measures. Its deficit is lower than Spain's but its debt is larger and its growth weaker. If a stigma is attached to a precautionary line of credit, Portugal might yet be pushed into a second bail-out.

The wooden union

After a long pause caused by the German election in September 2013, which saw Merkel returned to power at the head of a grand coalition with the Social Democrats, the euro zone resumed work on banking union in the autumn of 2013. At its heart, banking union requires trust. Germany must feel able to share liabilities for everybody's banks. And all countries must agree to stop coddling their banks so that more pan-European lenders can emerge.

Legal work on the single supervisor was finalised in November. It was due to be fully operational a year later, with Danièle Nouy, secretary-general of France's bank and insurance supervisor, as its first boss. The next stage, potentially involving public money, was more difficult: the creation of a single resolution mechanism to wind up or restructure bust banks. Germany had stubbornly opposed a central authority with access to pooled funds (levied from the banks), pushing instead for a network that would leave German money in German hands. Wolfgang Schäuble, reappointed as German finance minister after the election, had said in May that the euro zone should start with a "timber-framed" banking union; a steel one would require changing the treaties.[8] But with the approach of an end-of-year deadline, Germany began to shift.

First, common bail-in rules that would apply to all EU countries – whether in or out of the euro zone – were approved in December. These would ensure there could not be another Cyprus-style fiasco. Shareholders and bondholders would have to take the first losses – up to 8% of the bank's total assets – before any resolution funds could committed. Thereafter there would be a clear hierarchy of creditors, so that senior bondholders would take the hit before depositors, and deposits below €100,000 would be protected at all times.

Then Schäuble made an important concession. The joint euro-zone resolution fund would start with national "compartments", but over a ten-year period these would be progressively pooled until there was a single European fund of about €55 billion ($60 billion). In other words, he agreed to mutualise the money of German banks, if not yet that of German taxpayers. And Germany's answer to the question of trust was to give the new supervisor time to root out the problems. The principle could one day be applied to other reforms: how about the phased introduction of Eurobonds? For now, Schäuble's legal nitpicking produced a complex legal structure (mixing EU treaty provisions for the single market with an inter-governmental treaty). The decision-making process to wind up a bank would be almost comically convoluted, raising worries about whether a failing bank could really be dealt with over a weekend.

After some brinkmanship, the European Parliament and Council agreed a compromise on March 20th 2014, concluding banking union in just two years. MEPs objected to inter-governmentalism but relented because the alternative was to have no resolution mechanism at all. In return they obtained some streamlining of decision-making. With backing from the ECB, they shortened the period for the pooling of funds (from ten to eight years) and permitted the fund to borrow money on the markets. All knew that if the issue were not settled before the May 2014 European elections, it risked being delayed indefinitely.

Despite heady talk of "a revolution", banking union remained incomplete. There was still no single deposit-guarantee scheme. The promise of direct recapitalisation was remote: first losses had to be borne by shareholders and creditors; the burden would then be taken up by governments and only in extremis by the euro-zone rescue fund. The most glaring flaw was the lack of a common backstop, left to be decided at a future date. In the transition, national treasuries would step in if the resolution fund ran out of money; only if the burden threatened to ruin a country could it turn to the ESM. The obvious solution, to allow the ESM to extend a line of credit to the resolution fund, as the US Treasury does to the FDIC, was rejected by Germany. Saving taxpayers' money is a laudable aim. But banking union cannot be credible without some assurance that taxpayers collectively stand behind it if a big crisis strikes.

Banking union did not live up to the promise to help Spain or Ireland in the current crisis. Nor will it be much use should the new supervisor find large holes in the banks when it publishes the results of a thorough examination of bank balance sheets at the end of 2014. At best, and only if done properly, banking union could help prevent and lower the cost of a future crisis. For the foreseeable future banking union, like the currency union itself, will remain a timber-framed construction.

Beware of Europhoria

After the long crisis, markets seemed in the grip of "Europhoria" by early 2014, particularly as their worries shifted to emerging economies. The elation was probably overdone. The euro zone was hardly in good health.

The euro zone stopped shrinking in the first half of 2013 but was forecast to grow only slowly in 2014, when just Cyprus and Slovenia were still expected to be in recession. A weak recovery left the euro zone vulnerable to another slump. Unemployment in the periphery remained at worryingly high levels. Financial markets had been fragmented by the crisis, with firms in the periphery of the euro zone paying higher rates of interest for their loans – that is, when credit could be obtained at all – than equivalent companies in "core" economies. Comparable business on either side of, say, the border between Italy and Austria could pay markedly different interest rates on bank loans, as Figure 6.3 shows.

Beyond this, the danger of Japan-style deflation began to worry policymakers by early 2014, as the inflation rate for the euro zone as a whole slowed to 0.7% in February, well below the ECB's already conservative target of holding inflation in the medium term at close to but below 2%. Falling prices – already a reality in Greece, Cyprus, Portugal and Slovakia – hamper recovery, prompt consumers to postpone purchases in expectation of lower prices and increase the burden of debt on national economies. As Christine Lagarde, the IMF boss, put it in January 2014: "If inflation is the genie, then deflation is the ogre that must be fought decisively."

Two issues, in particular, highlighted the fragility of the euro zone's

FIG 6.3 **The north–south gap**
Interest on loans to non-financial corporations up to €1m, 2007–14, %

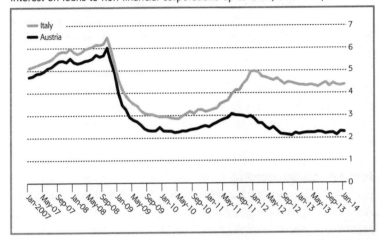

Source: ECB

condition. First was the oldest and most intractable problem: Greece. Astonishingly, poor blighted Greece made it to a primary budget surplus (before interest) at the end of 2013, for once exceeding expectations, thanks in part to a bumper tourist season. This was despite losing a quarter of its economic output since the start of the crisis, and with 27% of its workforce unemployed. In Germany, Samaras was being hailed as one of the saviours of the euro. This should have brought closer the promised day when the euro zone would ease its burden of debt, forecast to reach 176% of GDP at the end of 2013.

But at the beginning of 2014, just as Greece took over the rotating presidency of the EU, things started to sour again. Germany said it would not talk of dealing with Greece's debt until the second half of the year, that is, until after the European election. The delay might help the German government stem the rise of the new anti-euro Alternative for Germany party, but would make it harder for Samaras to resist the more dangerous charge of the radical leftist party, Syriza, which was leading in opinion polls. Moreover, the negotiations with the troika, in particular the IMF, got badly stuck.

On the face of it, the argument with the troika was about whether

Greece should continue the long years of fiscal consolidation. Greece had a short-term problem, with a small gap in its financing requirements in the second half of 2014, and a longer-term problem over how to reach a primary budget surplus of 4.5% of GDP by 2016, as foreseen in its troika programme.

Samaras, having survived thus far with an ever-shrinking parliamentary majority, announced he could no longer take any across-the-board austerity measures. Henceforth, his government said, the budding recovery should not be stifled; Greece would simply grow its way to the promised surplus. For veterans of the IMF, still defensive about having badly misjudged the first Greek bail-out, optimistic growth forecasts did not amount to a credible policy.

Beneath the question of how much more belt-tightening Greece would require lay deeper problems. One was whether Greece's debt relief, if and when it was agreed, should be in the form of a write-off in the nominal value of the debt, or whether softening the terms of its already soft loans by extending maturities and reducing interest would be good enough. The IMF thought a write-off would boost confidence among investors; the creditor countries said that was politically unacceptable. So "extend and pretend" seemed likely to win.

A more worrying issue was that Greece, even though it had largely complied with the demands of fiscal consolidation, was far behind in its promises to enact structural reforms and privatise state assets. Some of these had an impact on fiscal matters. But the more important ones had to do with liberalising the country's sclerotic economy to release its growth potential.

Greece has sharply cut its unit-labour costs, but mostly by reducing wages rather than by raising productivity. And despite the fall in labour costs, Greek exports were falling once the murky trade in fuel and volatile tourism revenues were stripped out of the data. This was alarming. In Spain, Portugal and Ireland lower labour costs boosted exports. Some Greeks blamed a lack of credit. Others noted that the country's main export market, the EU, had been in recession. But the real problem was an economy that produced few tradable goods. Greece had shot up the World Bank's ranks for the ease of starting firms; but in the wider measure of ease of doing business, it ranked 72nd in the world, behind Azerbaijan, Kyrgyzstan, Belarus and Kazakhstan. All this was evidence of a country still in need of far-reaching structural reform if it was to survive with a hard currency, at a time when its political system was running out of will for further change. European countries were pushing the IMF to give Greece a break, at least ahead of the European elections. But this was a particularly odd request, given the unwillingness of creditor countries to help Samaras by giving him early debt relief.

The other cloud over the euro zone was the future of Draghi's "whatever it takes" promise to intervene in bond markets through his policy of OMT. The long-delayed judgment by Germany's constitutional court was issued on February 14th, and it turned out to be a scathing denunciation of OMT. The court said it saw "important reasons to assume that it exceeds the European Central Bank's monetary policy mandate and thus infringes the powers of the member states, and that it violates the prohibition of monetary financing of the budget". The court refrained from telling German institutions to stop implementing the policy, but reserved the right to do so after referring the case to the European Court of Justice (ECJ). This bought OMT at least another year, and the ECJ may well support the ECB's contention that the policy falls within its remit. Nevertheless, the Karlsruhe court has introduced a note of doubt that may prove dangerous should the debt crisis ever reignite.

The changing balance of power

AS WELL AS CONSTITUTING THE MOST SERIOUS CHALLENGE to the European project since its inception, the euro crisis has had a huge impact on its political and economic balance, at every level. Among countries, it has hugely increased the influence of some, notably Germany, and decreased that of others, notably France. It has fostered a growing north–south divide in the European Union, which has to an extent replaced the previous east–west one. It has sharpened the division between those countries that are in the euro and those that are not. Among the EU institutions, it has strengthened the role of the European Council at the expense of the European Commission and the European Parliament. And although it has led to deeper integration of sorts, especially in fiscal policy, it has also reduced the political weight of the central EU bodies and increased that of national governments. Many if not all of these shifts in power will endure. Most will profoundly affect the workings of the wider EU as well as the euro zone.

Start with the institutions. Throughout the history of the European project, the balance of power among them and between them and national governments has altered, sometimes for structural reasons, sometimes as a reflection of individual personalities. In its early years the Commission was especially important: many new rules and directives were needed, there was no directly elected parliament and European leaders did not yet meet in the European Council. Yet the French president, Charles de Gaulle, who mistrusted the Commission and much preferred inter-governmentalism, was hugely important. It was de Gaulle who in 1965 precipitated the "empty chair" crisis when France refused to accept a treaty-prescribed move towards majority voting in the Council of Ministers. After a long French boycott of EU meetings, the eventual outcome was the 1966 Luxembourg compromise which, at least according to the French interpretation (now shared by the British), preserves the national veto if a country invokes its "vital national interests" even in legislation meant to be decided by the system of qualified-majority voting enshrined in the Rome treaty and later strengthened in the Single European Act.

The influence and power of later Commissions have fluctuated, but the institution reached its apogee under the presidency of Jacques Delors after 1984. He was a driving force behind both the single market and the single currency; indeed, in the late 1980s he turned into a hate-figure for British anti-Europeans (and for Margaret Thatcher) after he addressed the Trades Union Congress in 1988. He was hugely important for the adoption of EMU. Yet his influence in Brussels had diminished long before he stepped down from the job, somewhat disillusioned, in 1994.[1] And neither of his first two successors as Commission president, Jacques Santer and Romano Prodi, was able to re-establish the institution's previous pre-eminence.

When the Portuguese prime minister, José Manuel Barroso, took over as Commission president in 2004, he allied himself firmly with liberalising countries such as the UK, the Netherlands and, to a lesser extent, Germany (while not neglecting the interests of his own country). Under him the Commission has continued to play a crucial role in providing analysis, implementing the rules and drawing up legislative compromises, as well as protecting the interests of smaller countries and of a wider Europe. But it has proved hard to restore the Commission's political clout at a time of rising scepticism in public views of the European Union. Many national governments have come to see the Commission as too keen on petty regulation and too ready to appease the European Parliament, moving away from its supposedly neutral position between Parliament and Council – a perception that is likely to grow now that, under the Lisbon treaty, the Parliament has been given the explicit role of "electing" the Commission president after he or she has been nominated by heads of government.[2]

As the Commission's political influence has waned, the Parliament's has waxed. Besides its new role in the choice of a new president, the co-decision procedure for almost all legislation under the Lisbon treaty has given it extra powers. In its work on the new excessive-deficits procedure during the euro crisis, the Parliament played a positive role, especially over the new six- and two-pack legislation, which its economic and monetary affairs committee under a British MEP, Sharon Bowles, helped to shape. Yet national governments and EU leaders, even those traditionally keen to give the Parliament more powers, are nowadays increasingly disillusioned with it. This was especially obvious during repeated rows over the EU budget and the multi-annual financial framework during 2013: the Parliament's instinctive push for even more EU spending than the Commission had asked for won it few friends among net contributor countries. The growing presence of populist and extremist parties in the Parliament, while making it more representative, will not improve its image with national governments.[3]

The biggest winner from the euro crisis among the EU institutions has been the European Council of heads of state and government, because it brings together the 28 national leaders. That is partly because Herman Van Rompuy, the little-known, haiku-writing Belgian prime minister who was picked to be the European Council's first permanent president (and was promptly accused by Nigel Farage, leader of the UK Independence Party, of having "all the charisma of a damp rag and the appearance of a low-grade bank clerk"), has in fact proved an adept choice. As an economist from a euro-zone country, he was good at diagnosing the euro's ills; he has often pointed to the madness of not watching more carefully the rise in current-account deficits. From his background in Belgian politics he has also learnt the art of political compromise. His ability to speak English, French and German, shared also with Jean-Claude Juncker, who chaired the Eurogroup, has been useful. The jobs of European Council and Eurogroup summit president (which he added) have become more significant partly because of how he has done them. And, for the most part, he has forged a good working relationship with Barroso, with the Commission continuing to provide much of the technical and legal support for the work of the European Council.

The main reason the European Council is where the action now happens is that the euro crisis has increased the clout of national governments. This is largely because only national governments can command the resources needed to bail out excessively indebted countries or banks. It is also because, to raise the necessary money, most governments have needed to secure the consent of their national parliaments. In effect, the euro crisis has laid bare a tendency that could be detected long before 2009. This is that national governments and their leaders (with an increasingly large role played by finance ministers at the expense of foreign ministers, formerly the main actors in Brussels) have become the driving force of the euro zone and, by extension, of the EU as a whole.

Broad political power is thus shifting from the supranational European institutions and towards national governments thanks to the euro crisis. Yet at the same time many more intrusive powers are being vested at the EU level, because the euro zone has been forced to move in the direction of greater political as well as economic integration. The ECB is taking on the supervision of most euro-zone banks, for example, and it will also gain the power to require them to increase their capital or, in some cases, to shut them down. As part of the European semester, the Commission is getting extensive new monitoring powers, including the possibility of sanctions, over national budgets. The Parliament is arrogating to itself the job of scrutinising contracts for reform that are being debated and could yet be drawn up between national governments and Brussels. What explains the paradoxical combination of greater intrusive powers within the euro zone and the declining influence of the EU institutions?

Country-club rules

The answer is to be found in the shifting balance of power among EU countries, which is perhaps where the greatest impact of the euro crisis can be seen. The underlying fiction of the European project from the beginning was that member countries were broadly equal. Most institutions worked on the basis of one representative per country, although until the Nice treaty big countries were entitled to two commissioners. Admittedly, qualified-majority voting in the Council gave more weight to big than to small countries, but the system was still biased towards the small – and the most important decisions were almost always taken unanimously. Seats in the Parliament do reflect population size, but even there small countries have tended to be overrepresented (Malta has proportionately five times as many MEPs as Germany).

Yet despite all this, the notion of equality within the EU remains largely false. In practice, two countries have always acted as the principal engine in the European motor: France and Germany. Italy, the other big country in the original six, has never been able to match the clout of these two, partly because for many years its political system led to frequent elections and innumerable changes of prime minister, and partly because, after a long period of catch-up growth that lasted into the 1980s, its economic performance has been so dismal. Although the Netherlands has occasionally dissented, and has also in recent years turned noticeably more sceptical towards the European institutions, the Benelux trio have generally been willing to go along with Franco-German leadership. It has been hard for any newcomers, including largish countries such as the UK, Spain and Poland, to break in.

In the early years of the European project, especially after the Elysée treaty of 1963 that cemented links between the two countries, it was France that saw itself as in the lead politically, leaving the then West Germany to pay most of the bills. Indeed, this was one reason the French were reluctant to let the UK join in the early 1960s: in the words of the French foreign minister at the time, they did not want another cock on the dunghill. The EU institutions, including commissioners and their cabinets, were largely designed on French lines. The Commission's first secretary-general was French. The common agricultural policy, the common fisheries policy, the customs union and the budget were all drawn up in many ways to the benefit of the French at the expense of the Germans (and, sotto voce, of the British when they were eventually let into the club in 1973).

By then the relationship across the Rhine had become more one of equals, as (West) German economic power asserted itself. The response of successive French presidents and German chancellors was to forge still closer bilateral links, even though they often came from opposing political families: Valéry Giscard d'Estaing with Helmut Schmidt, François Mitterrand with Helmut Kohl, Jacques Chirac with

Gerhard Schröder. It became understood that, if France and Germany could agree on something, so (most of the time) could the rest. Even when the personal relationship was scratchy, the institutional bond between the two countries was close. The UK's attempts to insert itself into a possible trilateral relationship usually failed: the prime minister who came closest to pulling this off was Tony Blair, but his European credentials were tarnished when the UK declined to join the euro, and even more so when he later backed George Bush's war in Iraq, vehemently opposed by both the French and German leaders.

By this time, however, the Franco-German relationship was becoming more obviously lopsided. The turning point came with German unification in 1990, which made Germany significantly bigger than France both in population and in economic weight. That was indeed one reason Mitterrand pushed so hard for a single European currency: he hoped that it would give France more say in economic and monetary policy, which was increasingly being dictated for all EU members by the German Bundesbank. But as the years went by, it became ever more obvious that the Franco-German relationship had become a mechanism that was deployed to disguise German strength and French weakness.

There was a brief respite at the start of the euro when the German economy looked particularly weak, partly because Germany had joined the euro at a relatively high parity. *The Economist*, echoing Hans-Werner Sinn, a German economist, called Germany the sick man of Europe as recently as 2003.[4] But German industry responded to the challenge by determinedly cutting costs and holding down wages, while the Schröder government's Agenda 2010 reforms of the labour market and welfare system increased the German economy's flexibility. Rising demand from China for German-made machine tools and other products also boosted German exports. The result was that, by the time the euro crisis broke out openly in 2009–10, the gap in economic and financial strength between the two leading countries in the euro had become gapingly wide.

Germany's moment

This presented a big new challenge to the next incarnation of the dual leadership, after May 2007: Nicolas Sarkozy as French president and Angela Merkel as German chancellor. True to form and despite both coming from the centre-right, their relationship got off to a rocky start, not least because they were polar opposites in style. Sarkozy is a nervy, hyperactive showman. Merkel was a cautious, somewhat dour scientist. The two were known to find each other unbearable even though they had to work together – in English, no less, because neither spoke the other's language. They quickly clashed after Sarkozy became president when he floated plans for a new "Mediterranean Union" that appeared to be meant to exclude Germany. But it was the global financial crisis that really tested them.

At first France seemed to fare better during the crunch than Germany (and indeed the UK), with a much smaller loss of GDP in 2008–09.[5] Along with the British prime minister, Gordon Brown, Sarkozy played a big role in meetings of the G8 and G20 that tried to co-ordinate an international fiscal boost to stop the crisis turning an inevitable recession into a deep 1930s-style depression. At one point, he even cheekily announced to the press that France was acting while Germany was merely thinking about it. But when the euro crisis erupted in 2010 the structural weakness and relatively greater indebtedness of France compared with Germany soon became a huge problem.

Like so many of his predecessors, Sarkozy's response was to try to get closer to Merkel. He played up France's AAA rating as a key asset underpinning the successive rescue funds that had to be devised for Greece, Ireland, Portugal and later Spain and Cyprus. He and Merkel joined forces to suggest policy changes such as, at Deauville in October 2010, the involuntary involvement of the private sector in future debt restructurings. He pushed German-inspired fiscal austerity and did not press hard for an immediate agreement to the issuance of Eurobonds. The markets began to talk of "Merkozy" as the key tandem seeking to steer the euro zone out of its debt and growth crises. And the two leaders played a crucial role in 2011 in engineering the departures of Silvio Berlusconi in Italy and George

Papandreou in Greece and their replacement by technocrat-led governments.

Yet as the crisis dragged on, the pretence that France counted as much as Germany wore thin. Increasingly, it was the chancellery, the Bundestag and the German constitutional court in Karlsruhe, as well as public opinion in Germany, that were doing the most to determine the shape and speed of the euro zone's various rescue packages. As other countries, especially but not only those that had been bailed out, cut public spending, reduced budget deficits and pushed through structural reforms, an unchanged and unchanging France seemed to be turning into part of the problem rather than part of the solution. To Sarkozy's embarrassment, France lost its first AAA rating in early 2011. And then, in May 2012, he lost the presidential election to the Socialist candidate, François Hollande.

Hollande was a stronger pro-European than Sarkozy, as well as being easier to deal with on a personal level. Although he came from the opposite political camp to Merkel, he was on the right of his Socialist Party. Yet as the man who led the party when it split over the referendum on the EU's constitutional treaty in 2005, he was wary of any new treaty changes that the Germans might seek. Moreover, before his election he spoke out strongly against Merkel's austerity policies and in favour of more growth; he wanted to see some form of debt mutualisation, which was anathema to Merkel; and during the campaign he said next to nothing about the need for structural reforms or public-spending cuts at home, instead proposing tax increases, including a new 75% top rate of income tax.[6] After he came to power, far from seeking to reinvigorate the Franco-German axis, he tried to make common cause with the Italian and Spanish leaders in urging more growth-oriented policies in place of excessive austerity.

The response from Germany was frigid in the extreme. After two years of crisis-fighting, the last thing Merkel wanted was to see a weakened France deserting the "northern" camp of creditor countries like Germany, Austria, the Netherlands and Finland and joining instead the "southern" camp of debtors, whose instinctive answer to any problem was to borrow and spend more. France, it was noted darkly in Germany, had not balanced its budget since 1974.

One reason the Germans decided during 2012 that it would be too dangerous to let any country, even Greece, leave the euro was because they feared that it might lead to the currency eventually unravelling all the way up to the Rhine.

In short, France had now become, in German eyes, part of the problem and not of the solution. At a budget summit in February 2013 Hollande was so distant from the German position that he even failed to show up for a bilateral meeting with Merkel, something unheard of before. As one observer of EU summits noted, everybody always stopped to listen to Merkel; nobody paid any attention when Hollande took the floor, instead fiddling with their BlackBerries and iPhones. The marginalisation of France is also denting public opinion in that country, which is increasingly turning against both the euro and the EU. The French industry minister, Arnaud Montebourg, has taken to attacking the EU for its "free-market fundamentalism". Another striking example even among the pro-European elite was a 2013 book by François Heisbourg, from the Foundation for Strategic Research, in which he argued that the euro should be scrapped in order to preserve the European Union.[7]

Angela alone

In effect, Europe once again has what historians have called a German problem (with plenty of reason to hope that the solution will be more peaceful than in the past). The revival of a German problem is not at all comfortable for Merkel. Following the departure of Jean-Claude Juncker as prime minister of Luxembourg in late 2013 and of Estonia's Anders Ansip in 2014, she is the longest-serving national leader in the EU. With France so weak and Hollande so ineffectual, she is also the unchallenged head of the northern creditor camp in Europe. And with German unemployment and youth unemployment both at 20-year lows, GDP back above pre-crisis levels, a budget close to balance and a continuing huge current-account surplus, her country is the uncontested economic hegemon of Europe. France and Italy are, at best, bystanders; at worst, largely irrelevant.

Yet Germany remains a reluctant hegemon, not least for historical reasons. Its foreign and defence policies are inward-looking, commercially driven and instinctively pacifist, unlike the UK's and France's. Merkel may enjoy wielding power in Europe, and being seen by the rest of the world as the continent's most important leader, but neither she nor her country is entirely happy being treated too openly as such. Post-war German chancellors have traditionally seen more Europe as the answer to the German problem. But to critics of Merkel, especially during the euro crisis, her call for more Europe has often seemed like a call for a more German Europe, an effort to transform all euro-zone countries into mini-Germanys. The sensitivity this arouses was well demonstrated in November 2011 when a public claim by Volker Kauder, chairman of the Bundestag's foreign affairs committee, that "suddenly, Europe is speaking German" was swiftly disowned by most of his colleagues.[8]

Germany, in short, remains highly attuned to outside criticism. It also has many blind spots economically. This not only embraces the crude caricatures of Merkel with a moustache and talk of a new Third Reich that are seen and heard in Greece and elsewhere. It also includes more serious complaints from the likes of the IMF and the US Treasury that Germany relies too much on exports and too little on domestic consumption for growth; and that, by running such a large current-account surplus, determinedly holding down wages and failing to generate sufficient internal demand, the Germans contributed to the problems of the euro zone in the first place.

Such claims are vigorously rejected in Germany. Ever since the Greek crisis erupted in late 2009, the Germans have seen two roots of the problem: fiscal profligacy and a loss of competitiveness. On this diagnosis, the cure for the first is public-spending cuts and tax rises; for the second, it is structural reforms to labour and product markets to reduce unit labour costs and restore competitiveness. Germany has long kept its public finances under better control than others and it also pushed through the Agenda 2010 reforms in 2003. Other euro-zone countries simply have to copy this example. The notion that Germany might need to do more, for instance increasing wages or public spending, or boosting domestic investment, is often greeted with disbelief. German business, it is said in reply, must compete on a global stage; trying to rebalance within Europe by making it less competitive externally would be disastrous for the entire continent.

That the coalition agreement in Germany may have this effect, by introducing a high minimum wage and lowering the retirement age for certain workers, reflects politics rather than policy choices.

As Merkel has come increasingly to be the main or even only voice that counts in the euro crisis, she has also become more dubious about the value of the EU institutions. Admittedly, she has quietly sided with the ECB against criticisms from the Bundesbank, even when two of her most loyal lieutenants, Axel Weber and Jürgen Stark, resigned in protest. But she has dragged her feet on banking union, and her response to calls from the Commission or from other European countries for debt mutualisation has been cold. For her, keeping in line with public opinion at home and satisfying both the Bundestag and the constitutional court in Karlsruhe matter far more than any dreamy euro-federalist vision. She has at times been criticised by such predecessors as Helmut Kohl and Helmut Schmidt for this. The current coalition agreement suggests a number of changes to the Commission, including reducing its propensity to regulate.

It must be conceded that, at least for Merkel, this approach to Europe has worked wonders. For all the brickbats hurled at her, especially from abroad, for being too slow to move, too eager to impose austerity on the Mediterranean, too unwilling to boost demand at home and too leery of explaining to Germans how much they would lose if the euro were to break up, she has retained enormous popularity at home. Almost all other euro-zone countries have seen their leaders pushed out by voters as a result of the euro crisis. Merkel, however, took an impressive 42% of the vote in the federal election in September 2013, and she has since gone on to form a grand coalition with the Social Democrats that clearly leaves her and her finance minister, Wolfgang Schäuble, in charge of German policy on the euro. German voters, it seems, instinctively trust her both to do the right thing and to protect their interests.

Mediterranean angst, northern bravado

Worries about French weakness and about being lonely at the top have prompted the Germans to look around for other potential partners in the European Union. The UK is out, as it is seen as too semi-detached from the project. The Mediterranean countries are also broadly no good. Most of them have received help from European bail-out funds and are still struggling to comply with their reform programmes and sort out their banks. Spain is likely to be the first to come good but still faces severe economic and political difficulties. Only Ireland has become the German poster-child for how a bailed-out country can change itself.

Italy is the perpetual underperformer in the EU: a big economy, second only to Germany in manufacturing, but seemingly incapable of reforming itself to regain lost competitiveness. Alone among euro-zone countries its income per head is lower now than when the euro began in 1999. During his brief technocratic administration in 2011–12, Mario Monti promised to be a firm ally of Merkel's, and he tried, with only partial success, to push through structural reforms, including to pensions. But at EU meetings he tended to side with those criticising Germany for not doing enough to boost domestic demand and the ECB for failing to act to lower interest rates in the periphery. Italy has traditionally favoured ever-closer union in Europe, on the basis that many Italians prefer rule from Brussels to rule from Rome, but such an approach is now out of favour in Germany.

Monti was forced to call an election in February 2013 in which he did badly. After complex bargaining, Enrico Letta, the young deputy leader of Italy's centre-left Democratic Party, succeeded in putting together a broad coalition together with Berlusconi's People of Freedom (PdL) party and a scattering of centrists – the same broad coalition that had backed Monti. The country came out of its excessive deficit procedure in June, giving Letta a political boost, but Italy's politics remained as dysfunctional as ever. Letta found it no easier to enact reforms than did Monti. He survived an attempt by Berlusconi to bring down the government in October, just before the old rogue lost his parliamentary immunity following conviction on charges of fraud. Berlusconi's move backfired; instead of bringing down the government, his own PdL party split, with a faction of moderates sticking with Letta. But Letta then faced a deadlier challenge from his own side. The turbo-charged former mayor of Florence, Matteo Renzi, took over the leadership of the Democratic Party in December, and then pushed Letta out of power in February 2014.

Like Monti, Letta had been popular with Merkel partly because he was not Berlusconi and partly because he understood the case for structural reforms at home. But Merkel was never confident of seeing much in the way of radical reform from his baggy left-right coalition. It remains to be seen what she will make of Renzi. This young and energetic new leader is now widely seen both inside and outside Italy as the last great hope of his country's reformers. But his coalition is not much stronger than Letta's, and he is vulnerable to the charge of being yet another unelected leader imposed on Italian voters.

That leaves the northern group in the euro zone, most of which are natural allies of Germany. Austria, Finland and Luxembourg are the only other AAA-rated countries that help to sustain the rating of euro-zone rescue funds. But all are small. The Dutch and Finns usually support German calls for austerity. Yet the Netherlands was downgraded in 2013 as the Dutch economy struggled to overcome the after-effects of a housing bust. The eastern newcomers to the euro, Slovakia, Slovenia, Estonia and (from January 2014) Latvia, are small countries as well, and Slovenia has hovered on the brink of needing a bail-out for its indebted banks. However, these two groups give powerful support to the broad German narrative, which is that the cure for the euro crisis is to be found in fiscal austerity and structural reform at home. The Baltic countries, especially Latvia, went through almost as wrenching an adjustment in the early 2000s as Greece, and without provoking riots. They are among the strongest advocates that other heavily indebted countries should follow suit. Latvia's is now the fastest-growing economy in the EU.

What the euro crisis has clearly done is to break what used to be the EU's east–west division. Most of the countries that joined in 2004, and even more so Bulgaria and Romania, which joined in 2007, remain significantly poorer than the others, but they are catching up as they benefit from EU structural funds. The new economic and political division in Europe is increasingly a north–south one. This is potentially troubling for the entire project. For its first 50 years until 2007, it always functioned on the basis that it was bringing about convergence between member countries. Since the euro crisis hit, the pattern has been more one of divergence. And that could easily stir up still more popular resentment of the EU in the south.

Germany is also looking to some non-euro countries as potential new partners, especially Poland and, to a lesser extent, Sweden. Indeed, were Poland to join the single currency, it is not too fanciful to see it vying with France and the UK as Germany's main allies (French suspicion of eastern enlargement was often attributable to its worry about losing influence within the club to Germany). Bilateral German–Polish relations are warmer than they have been in 500 years. Merkel respects Donald Tusk, the Polish prime minister, so much that she briefly toyed with putting him forward for the Commission presidency. Radek Sikorski, the foreign minister, has been widely touted as a candidate for one of the top EU jobs, at least since his notable November 2011 speech in Berlin when he announced that he was "probably the first Polish foreign minister in history to say this, but here it is: I fear German power less than I am beginning to fear German inactivity".[9]

The increasing influence of Poland does, however, throw the spotlight on the remaining big division in the EU, besides an economic north–south one. This is between the 18 euro-zone ins and the ten outs. As the euro zone pursues deeper political integration, including of fiscal policy and banking regulation, and even toys with setting up its own separate institutions, it is becoming increasingly clear that the single currency is the most important subgroup in the broader European club. That raises huge dangers for the maintenance of the wider single market at 28, and especially for the position of the most recalcitrant country of all: the UK.

8 In, out, shake it all about

UNTIL EUROPEAN ECONOMIC AND MONETARY UNION (EMU) came along with the Maastricht treaty, the general assumption was that all members of the European club would participate in all its formations and policies. Naturally there were exceptions: Ireland was neutral, so when it joined in 1973 it became the only member not in NATO; and the UK and Ireland stayed out of attempts to set up passport-free travel through the Schengen treaty. Some inner clubs such as the Benelux trio also existed. But Maastricht marked the first occasion when some EU countries, in this case first the UK and later Denmark, specifically opted out of a treaty obligation to join a major European project, the single currency. Also in Maastricht, the UK opted out of the so-called social chapter of social and employment legislation. Moreover, the treaty clearly envisaged that not all European Union members would qualify for EMU. Thus was born a new concept for the European project: that most were in but some would stay out of certain projects.

The newcomers to the European club in 1973, followed by Greece in 1981 and, to a lesser extent, Spain and Portugal in 1986, had long been an irritant to the more fervent Europhiles from the original six, especially those who believed that they were committed to a path that would lead to a federal United States of Europe. By joining the then EEC, all countries accepted the goal set out in the preamble to the Treaty of Rome, of an "ever closer union". But, except for Ireland and, later, Spain and Portugal, all of them were more or less unenthusiastic about this objective. The UK especially came to be seen, notably during the years of Margaret Thatcher, as a backslider in Europe and an increasingly Eurosceptic country. That became even

more obvious during the painfully protracted process of ratification
of the Maastricht treaty by the British Parliament in the years of the
John Major government between 1992 and 1994.

This perception, combined with the simple fact of the European
Union then comprising 12 rather than six members (soon to become
15, after the accession of Austria, Finland and Sweden in 1995), led
some to ponder the merits of a Europe that would move at different
speeds or even towards different destinations. The idea that a small
group of countries might go faster than others had been floated as
far back as the 1970s by Leo Tindemans, then Belgian prime minister,
but without finding favour.[1] In 1994 two leading German Christian
Democrats, Wolfgang Schäuble (who became the German finance
minister in 2009) and Karl Lamers, published a paper in which they
revived the notion by suggesting that, rather than always being forced
to go at the pace of the slowest, a "hard core" of countries might move
ahead with deeper integration, letting the backmarkers catch up later
(or perhaps not at all).[2]

The concept was taken a stage further in the 1997 Amsterdam treaty.
Denmark, Ireland and the UK insisted on the right to opt out of future
justice and home affairs laws if they wanted to. And a new treaty
provision was approved that specifically provided for the possibility
of "enhanced co-operation", meaning that a subset of EU members
could go ahead with steps towards greater integration without having
to wait for all to agree. By this time the notion had acquired many
different labels. Besides hard cores and enhanced co-operation, these
included variable geometry, avant-garde, pioneer groups, flexibility,
concentric circles, multi-speed, two-speed, multi-tier, two-tier. The
exact label used often depended on its user's views: integrationists
tended to prefer language that implied different classes or speeds of
EU membership, whereas the British (and Danes) generally preferred
wording that simply connoted variations in the terms of a country's
membership.

For most areas of EU policy, having some countries in but others
out can be seen as a detail, perhaps a slight annoyance, but not
otherwise a huge issue. There are few real concerns in Europe over
the UK and Ireland insisting, as islands that lack compulsory identity
cards, that they want to stay out of the Schengen passport-free zone,

which anyway includes such non-EU countries as Norway and Switzerland. Similarly, nobody worries much that Denmark does not participate in most EU military or defence-related activities. The Amsterdam provisions for enhanced co-operation themselves have been used only twice, for a measure on divorce and for the EU patent (which Italy and Spain refused to join on linguistic grounds), without upsetting the entire system.

EMU is, however, more serious, mainly because it so strongly affects other European policies. Of course it was always going to be a club within a club, since the Maastricht criteria were designed from the start to restrict membership of the single currency to those that qualified. Greece failed in 1998, for example, though as the Commission said in its opinion on the matter it arguably still failed most of the criteria when it joined in 2001. But some countries that could have signed up for stage three of EMU (adopting the single currency) deliberately chose not to. The UK and Denmark had treaty opt-outs. Although Tony Blair seemed for a time hopeful of joining after he became prime minister in 1997, his chancellor of the exchequer, Gordon Brown, was against. The "five tests" that Brown devised for membership (on business cycles, flexibility, investment, financial services and growth) may have been more sensible than the Maastricht criteria, but they also proved impossible to pass. Denmark put the matter to a referendum in September 2000, which returned a negative majority. Sweden, which was legally obliged to join by the terms of its accession treaty, chose also to put the issue to its people, who voted no in September 2003. Thus the euro began life with three "voluntary" non-members from the EU.

All countries that accede to the European Union are now legally required by their accession treaties also to join the euro (something that would apply, incidentally, to an independent Scotland). But they have to take the step only when they are ready and when they meet the Maastricht criteria. In practice, this has meant that no country can be forced into the euro if it chooses not to adopt it. Moreover, the process was always going to take some time for the mainly central and eastern European countries that joined the EU in 2004 and 2007. Slovenia was the first new entrant to join the euro, in 2007. It has since been followed by Cyprus and Malta (2008), Slovakia (2009), Estonia

(2011) and Latvia (2014). This means that 18 of the European Union's 28 member countries are also members of the euro, while ten remain, at least for now, outside the single currency.[3]

When in trumps out

This division into ins and outs is, of course, somewhat blurred and fluid. Because it shadows the euro and the ECB so closely, Denmark already functions as if it is in, though it would need another referendum before it could actually join – and that seems unlikely for now. But most of the "outs" are, in effect, "pre-ins". Lithuania will clearly follow the other two Baltic republics into the euro as soon as it can, probably in 2015. Poland will take quite a lot longer, but its intention to join at some point is clear. Bulgaria, Romania and Croatia may well need a long period before they are deemed ready to take on the euro's obligations. Of the recent entrants, only the Czech Republic and perhaps Hungary seem to be unsure in principle whether to join the euro, putting them closer to the same camp as Sweden and the UK.

Why does any of this matter? There are three broad answers. The first is that, as the euro crisis has pushed its members towards deeper integration, so it has inexorably started to make membership of the single currency more important than any other aspect of the European Union. As noted in previous chapters, in the four years to 2014 the task of saving the euro has been overwhelmingly the main European business for Germany's Angela Merkel, as for other euro-zone leaders. Similarly, the pressure on bailed-out countries to comply with creditors' demands for fiscal retrenchment and structural reforms has overwhelmed any other EU actions and policies. Although the two are in practice often conflated, to citizens of Greece or Portugal it is the euro and not the EU that is seen to have made their lives a misery. Yet it is the EU, not the single currency, against which they tend to fulminate most loudly (opinion polls in most countries continue to find majorities for staying in the euro).

Second, institutional and other changes adopted by and for the euro can have a direct impact on the structure of the wider club, sometimes to the latter's disadvantage. The emergence of the

Eurogroup, which was fiercely resisted by most of the outs, especially the UK, has clearly reduced the significance of EcoFin meetings of finance ministers, just as the outs predicted. Now euro summits threaten to do the same to European Councils, one reason why Donald Tusk, the Polish prime minister, greeted their establishment with bitter words, addressed to Merkel, "Are we getting in your way? You are humiliating us." Other institutional changes over recent years, including the setting-up of the euro zone's various bail-out funds, the fiscal compact treaty and the banking union, under which bank supervision for euro-zone countries is moving to the ECB, will not apply to several countries not in the euro. Future ideas could go even further: a euro-zone budget or insurance fund, or a separate euro-zone Commission and Parliament, would clearly downgrade the role and significance of their wider EU equivalents.

Third, and related to this, the euro and the policies adopted for it can affect policies that touch on all EU countries, including outs. The most obvious risk is that decisions taken by the euro zone on issues like taxation could spill into or even damage the wider single market. Under the provisions of the Lisbon treaty, from 2015 onwards the 18 euro-zone countries will constitute a "qualified majority" in themselves. This means that if they were to form a caucus before meetings of the full 28-member Council of Ministers, they could, in effect, take a decision that would then willy-nilly be imposed on the rest. In recognition of this, the UK insisted that in the European Banking Authority, which is based in London, decisions should be taken by a "double majority" system that protects the position of outs by requiring measures to have majority support of both groups – though as more outs join the euro, this system will lose much of its potency and it will stop working altogether when fewer than four countries are out.

A couple of considerations make these three points more worrying for the future. The first is that there is a subtle ideological difference between the 18 ins and the ten outs. The first group has a slightly more protectionist, anti-free market bent, largely because it counts the Mediterranean countries and France among its most important members. By contrast, the outs include almost all of the EU's most liberal free traders, including the UK, Denmark and Sweden from older members and Poland and the Czech Republic from newer ones.

Merkel for one is fully aware of this, which is why she has always remained keen to preserve single-market policy decisions for the full 28, not the narrower 18, a group in which she has fewer natural allies.[4]

The second consideration is that the divide between ins and outs is likely to persist for some time, and conceivably forever. When any of the outs have raised concerns about being disadvantaged by their status, one easy response has always been to point to a simple solution to their worries: they should join the euro. And indeed, as already noted, many of the outs are pre-ins that are planning to do just that. But the euro crisis has made several countries extremely nervous about plunging in too soon. It has also led the ins to be more careful about whom they admit – many now believe that it was a mistake to let in Greece, for example. Some of the outs, including Sweden and Denmark, must also win referendums before they can join. Above all, there is one out, indeed the biggest of them all, that is highly unlikely to join the euro for the foreseeable future, if ever: the UK.

Those pesky Brits

It may seem odd for a book looking mainly at the causes and consequences of the euro crisis to devote much space to a country that has no intention of adopting it. But the ills of the single currency and how they are resolved could have a profound effect on the UK debate about whether to stay in the club. And that debate in turn will affect the euro zone, for it is hard to see either it or the wider EU going ahead unaffected if a huffy UK were to pick up its toys and walk out, which has become a distinct possibility.

The UK has always been the most awkward member of the European club. This goes back at least as far as Churchill's 1946 Zurich speech, when he called for a more politically integrated Europe but made clear that the UK would not be part of it, as well as to the detachment of the British representative at the 1956 Messina conference. It was only in 1961 that the British government decided it should get more involved, but by then France was led by de Gaulle, who implacably (if, perhaps, understandably, on the grounds that the UK had interests that were more Atlanticist than continental) twice vetoed British entry – to the chagrin of the other five members.

Even after Edward Heath triumphantly took the UK into the EEC in 1973, its reputation as a reluctant member endured. His Labour opponent, Harold Wilson, had opposed the entry terms and, when he won election in 1974, set about what he called a "renegotiation", largely as a political gesture meant to appease his party's fiercest anti-marketeers (a tale that may sound familiar to observers of the British Conservative Party 40 years on). He knew that he could not push the idea too far, however, so he stopped short of calling for further treaty changes and settled for mostly cosmetic measures that were enough to secure an overwhelming yes vote for continuing membership in a referendum held in June 1975.

This by no means ended British grumpiness, however. After it lost the 1979 election, the Labour Party moved into a strong anti-European position. Under the leadership of Michael Foot from 1980, it campaigned for (and lost) the 1983 election on a manifesto promising immediate withdrawal from the EEC. But Europeans did not find the nominally pro-European Tory government elected in 1979 an easy partner, either. Margaret Thatcher began her time as prime minister by demanding her money back from the European budget and ended it 11 years later by crying "no, no, no" to suggestions that the European project might evolve towards a closer federal union, with the Commission acting as a government, the Parliament as a lower chamber and the Council of Ministers as an upper house – an incident that contributed directly to the rebellion within the party which led to her removal from office.

So it has been with the UK and the single currency, almost from its beginnings, and to an extent so it is today. From the original opt-out at Maastricht, which John Major, Thatcher's successor, secured, until the establishment of the euro in 1999, the British government and public have remained deeply dubious about both the wisdom of setting it up and its prospects of survival. Indeed, in 1994 Major himself expressed his scepticism about the chances of the single currency ever coming into being: writing in *The Economist*, he talked of those who continued to recite the mantra of full EMU as having "all the quaintness of a rain dance and about the same potency".[5] When the euro duly arrived five years later, many Britons were surprised – and they were even more astonished when it survived its first ten years.

Against this background, it was to be expected that most British observers, and even many British politicians, reacted differently from the rest of Europe to the eruption of the euro crisis in 2009. With a strong feeling of "I told you so", many appeared at first to welcome the single currency's travails and to forecast its early demise. Since the UK had long warned against the folly of the euro, it chose – unlike, say, Poland and Sweden – to distance itself from most rescue packages for individual countries (save that for Ireland, with which the UK has obvious strong links) as well as to stand aside from any institutional or treaty-based response. That the euro crisis coincided with the arrival of a new Tory-Liberal coalition led by David Cameron in May 2010 made the British position even tougher, for since the mid-1990s the Conservatives have taken over from Labour as the mainstream party that most loves to hate Europe.

Indeed, Cameron has been under pressure from his Eurosceptic backbenchers to do something on Europe ever since he became prime minister. As a candidate for the party leadership in 2005, he had promised to pull out of the European People's Party, the main transnational centre-right political group, and did so in 2009, annoying Merkel in particular, as well as weakening both his and his country's influence in the EU. He also promised to put the new Lisbon treaty to a referendum, but later abandoned that pledge because the treaty had been ratified by the time he took office. Instead he passed the European Union Act, which requires that any further EU treaty that transfers significant powers to Brussels must be approved by a national referendum.

The Cameron government also took a different attitude from its Labour predecessor towards efforts to resolve the euro crisis. Although it stuck firmly to the principle that it was, essentially, none of the UK's business and thus not for the UK to join in helping to solve, it quickly grasped that a meltdown of the euro would be highly damaging to the British as well as to the European economies. So from quite an early stage Cameron and his chancellor of the exchequer, George Osborne, urged the euro zone to take whatever steps were necessary to resolve the crisis, including pushing for deeper political and fiscal integration from which the UK would stand aside. This was a big change from traditional British policy, which had always been to remain as closely involved as possible in all EU and euro-zone actions, often in the hope of slowing them down as much as possible.

This was still, however, not enough for Cameron's Eurosceptic backbenchers. Frightened also by the growing appeal of Nigel Farage's UK Independence Party (UKIP), which stood explicitly for withdrawal from the European Union, they still craved some kind of confrontation. They were granted their wish in December 2011 when the European Council wished to adopt the fiscal compact, a treaty cementing new rules on fiscal policy and also requiring national governments to insert "debt brakes" limiting budget deficits into their constitutions. Cameron came to Brussels threatening to veto this treaty unless he was given assurances protecting the City of London from possible future changes in financial regulations. Yet when he tabled his suggestions, the other governments ignored his request and simply adopted the fiscal compact as an inter-governmental treaty outside the normal EU framework. Nor did Cameron win much support in his refusal to sign up: ultimately 25 countries ratified the fiscal compact, including eight non-euro members, leaving only the UK and the Czech Republic as non-signatories (although the Czechs now plan to sign too).

Even that was not the end of Cameron's European adventures. He took the hardest possible line on negotiations over the 2014–20 EU budget that went by the unlovely name of the "multiannual financial framework". Rather than reopening the question of what the EU budget was for and whether it could be spent more efficaciously, a goal that might have been easier to achieve had he been willing to give up some of the UK rebate, he set himself the public goal of simply cutting the budget in real terms. With support from Merkel, he eventually got his way, but at the price not just of preserving farm spending broadly intact but also annoying both the European Parliament and potential central European allies like Poland.

The budget wrangle did little to improve the mood of Eurosceptics in the Tory party. They still wanted some commitment to renegotiate the UK's membership and promise voters an in/out referendum. Cameron fended off the pressure for as long as he could, but eventually he felt that he had to set out his plans. In his so-called Bloomberg speech in January 2013 (given in London after repeated failed efforts to find a suitable continental location), he called for substantial reforms to the EU, including less regulation, a completion of the single market, a more growth-enhancing agenda and a streamlined bureaucracy. He rejected the idea that the UK might adopt the Norwegian or Swiss options of being outside the EU but subject to most of its rules. He suggested a bigger role for national parliaments and some (unspecified) passing of powers back from European to national level. Although he carefully avoided specific British demands, he announced the establishment of a new audit of EU competences to see whether and where policy areas had stretched too much (thus far it has found remarkably few cases). And he added that at the next election his party would campaign for these reforms to be made by 2017 and, on the basis of a reformed EU, put the issue of the UK's continuing membership to a referendum.[6]

Back to ins and outs

This is where the UK's argument over its future impinges both on the future of the euro and on the relationship between ins and outs. Cameron may not win enough votes in 2015 to form a single-party government, so his threat to hold a referendum in 2017 may become moot. Both the other main party leaders are refusing to offer a referendum unless there is a substantial new treaty transferring powers to Brussels, but pressure on them is likely to grow. Either way, questions about the UK's continuing membership are likely to persist. Yet the attention of most other European leaders will continue to be focused more on fixing the euro crisis than on what sort of concessions to keep the UK in the EU might be acceptable.

Most EU leaders, especially Merkel, would like to keep the UK in. Moreover, several countries, including the Netherlands, Sweden and Denmark as well as Germany, are sympathetic to much of Cameron's agenda. There is a general desire to cut back excessive EU regulation and to rein in the European Commission and European Parliament. Yet there is a limit to the changes other countries might be willing to make to keep the UK in, and certainly no desire to give it special opt-outs or other arrangements that might benefit one country at the apparent expense of others. And there is a concern that, whatever is offered to the UK, its voters might choose to leave the EU anyway, an eventuality that somewhat weakens British bargaining power in negotiating a new deal.

What might clinch that outcome is any growth in feeling that the euro-zone ins are determined to go ahead with integrationist measures, including possibly further changes applying to them alone, that ignore the wishes or interests of non-euro countries. By not joining the euro, the British government has shown itself to be content to be in the outer circle of a Europe of concentric circles. But that does not inevitably have to mean being left on the fringes of all policy- and decision-making. In his first big speech on Europe in January 2014, Osborne expressed his own concerns about the outs being discriminated against, adding that without reform, the UK might face the choice between joining the euro, which it would never do, and leaving the EU. Perhaps ironically, given this worry, he also suggested that in some cases actions to deepen the single market could be taken by using enhanced co-operation.[7]

If the outs are to feel protected, however, policies in areas as diverse as the single market, the environment, taxation, trade and transport should largely continue to be made at 28, as more obviously should foreign and security policy. If Merkel and her allies accept the idea of making policy in any of these areas at 18, the risk of the UK's exit from the broader EU can only increase, as Osborne argued. The broader worries of the outs would increase as well. The French "Eiffel" group has proposed strengthening euro-zone institutions, making this problem potentially even worse. All this suggests that an important part of the agenda for euro-zone countries in the next few years should be a better arrangement of relations between ins and outs.

The fear of outs that in future policies may be made by ins without their having much or even any say echoes a broader fear of voters: that increasingly the European Union and the euro zone are deciding matters without sufficient democratic control. As the euro zone integrates further and more intrusively, it is running into a huge potential row about the legitimacy and democratic accountability of its actions. Indeed, it is this, rather than the financial markets, that could pose one of the biggest risks to the EU's future.

9 Democracy and its discontents

THE NOTION THAT THERE IS A DEMOCRATIC DEFICIT in Europe is almost as old as the European project itself. Until 1979, when the first elections to the European Parliament were held, none of the European institutions were directly elected, and the gap between ordinary citizens and decisions taken in Brussels was seen to be a yawning one. National governments, which are elected, are of course represented in the Council of Ministers, the senior legislative body. But most have tended to keep quiet about their bargaining and few are held to account for actions in Brussels by their own national parliaments. Moreover, the spread of qualified-majority voting has meant that individual governments can now be forced to accept policies that they have themselves opposed.[1]

Over time, various suggestions have been made for filling this democratic deficit. Increasing the powers of the European Parliament is one that has been pursued through almost every treaty. Greater transparency in both the Commission and the Council has long been another favourite. Greater democratic input into the Council of Ministers through national parliaments has often been urged. So sometimes has the idea of some body that more directly involves national legislatures. And there is increasing recourse to referendums to approve new treaties: no fewer than ten were promised for the abortive constitutional treaty, compared with just one for the Single European Act of 1987.

None of these has proved satisfactory as a remedy for the deficit. The European Parliament has continued to disappoint even its most ardent supporters. Transparency has been improved, but few ordinary citizens understand even the basics of how the EU works; indeed, most have no idea what the difference is between the Commission and the Council of Ministers. Most national parliaments remain bad at holding ministers to account for decisions made in Council meetings, and attempts to get them to work together have largely failed. As for referendums, almost as many have been lost as won, so most governments feel decidedly nervous about holding any more.

It is true that public scepticism about institutions has been as strong (or sometimes even stronger) at national as at European level. In many countries, the loss of faith in the European Parliament, for instance, is matched by a similar or even greater loss of belief in the efficacy of the national parliament. Moreover, in many countries duties that once devolved on directly elected governments – monetary policy, exchange-rate policy or competition policy, say – have been handed to unelected bodies on the basis that they will be done better. Yet there is still a bigger cause for concern when something similar happens at European level. Even when citizens are fed up with their own government or parliament, they do not question their legitimacy or their continuing existence. But when it happens at European level, which seems more foreign, many query both.

Following the national model, some commentators have accordingly suggested as an alternative that the European Union should rest on a different idea altogether: that of output rather than input legitimacy. On this basis, there is no real need to get hung up about democratic accountability as such. Rather, the European project can be expected to gain and retain public support – and thus end up acquiring greater legitimacy – simply by delivering good results. If voters can see that, thanks to the EU, their economies are more successful than they would be without it, they will be content. In this context it helps when there are concrete results from EU actions to point to: lower airfares or mobile-phone roaming charges, say.

Yet three related developments have largely kyboshed even this notion. The most obvious is that, far from being seen to deliver consistently good results, the European Union and especially the euro are now seen by large numbers of voters to be delivering mostly bad ones. Across much of the continent, Europe (and especially the single currency) is today associated with austerity, spending cuts, tax increases, rising joblessness and chronically slow growth. Debtor

FIG 9.1 **Disaffection**
Positive opinions of the EU, 2003–13, % polled

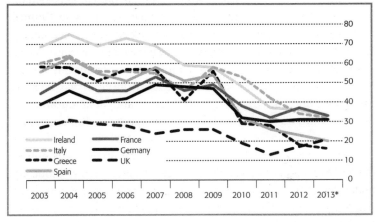

*Spring survey
Source: Eurobarometer autumn surveys

countries have seen a particularly sharp fall in enthusiasm for the European project as a result (see Figure 9.1). But even in creditor countries, which have suffered less economically, Europe and the euro have lost their appeal, because they are now associated with bail-outs and transfers rather than with rising prosperity.

This new mood music has become especially discordant for Europhiles. Their messages that the EU would boost growth through its single market, that the euro would improve competitiveness by promoting reform, and that both groups would protect European citizens from the pressure of globalisation and the fallout from the world financial crisis have fallen flat. Instead, Eurosceptics everywhere feel vindicated: their view that there is too much regulation by a remote EU bureaucracy and their warnings about the insanity of adopting a single currency without the right institutions, without moves towards political union and without enough democratic control seem to have been borne out by events.

The second consequential development has been a sharp fall in the popularity of the European project, right across Europe. Polls taken in 2013 by Eurobarometer, the German Marshall Fund and the

Pew Global Attitudes survey have all come up with similar findings.[2] Especially in the south, but also in the north, approval of the EU has declined fast in recent years. The number of people who consider their country's membership to be a good thing has also fallen. The decline has been most precipitate in Mediterranean countries like Spain and Greece. But it is also remarkable in France, where the latest Pew survey found an even smaller proportion of the population approving of the EU than in the traditionally Eurosceptic UK.

This sharp dip in the EU's popularity in opinion surveys is reflected in the rise of populist parties that are anti-euro and anti-EU. Some of these parties are from the far right, some from the far left. Often they are anti-free trade and anti-globalisation. In many cases they are strongly against immigration, which is increasingly associated with the EU because of its eastward expansion to take in not just the central European countries but also Bulgaria and Romania, for which free movement of labour arrived only in January 2014 (the British and some other governments are trying to curtail benefit entitlements for some specified groups of immigrants). Anti-Islam feelings also play a role. But their new-found strength owes most to the populists' ability to channel growing anti-EU sentiment.

Thus Greece has seen the rise not just of Golden Dawn, an explicitly extreme-right party, but also of Syriza, an anti-austerity left-wing party that is running ahead of the ruling New Democracy party in opinion polls. Spain and Portugal have, so far, escaped the rise of populist parties of the right, but the more extreme United Left party is doing well in Spain and support for the two mainstream centre-right and centre-left parties has collapsed. Italy has seen the spectacular rise of Beppe Grillo's Five Star movement, which took almost 25% of the vote in the election of February 2013, forcing the centre-left and centre-right parties into an uneasy coalition. In France, Marine Le Pen's National Front is running close to 20% in the opinion polls.

The rise of populists and extremists is not confined to troubled euro-zone countries alone. In Finland, the True Finns (now the Finns Party) under Timo Soini, which came out of nowhere in 2011, largely to protest against the euro, are scoring 20% or more in most opinion polls. In the Netherlands, Geert Wilders' Party of Freedom is also riding high. Wilders has formed an alliance with Le Pen for the

European elections, campaigning on an anti-EU, anti-euro platform. The UK Independence Party has refused to join this alliance, but it too has been scoring highly in the polls. Across central and eastern Europe a swathe of extremist and populist parties, from Jobbik in Hungary to the League of Catholic Families in Poland, are similarly doing well.

Almost the only country not to have seen a sharp upsurge in a populist, anti-euro or anti-EU party is Germany. It is also one of the few countries where the number of people with a favourable opinion of the EU has not fallen sharply in recent years. Residual German war guilt plays a part in holding down extremist parties. Yet it is, on the face of it, surprising that anti-EU or anti-euro sentiment has not made itself felt, as the German public has shown itself deeply hostile to the whole notion of bail-outs and transfers to Mediterranean countries. Moreover, a new party, Alternative for Germany, has been established and, although it narrowly failed to get into the Bundestag in the September 2013 election, its poll ratings have since been rising. The real reason Germany looks different from other countries may be that it has suffered little during the euro crisis. Besides, German voters have come to trust Merkel not to let them down.

The search for legitimacy

The third and perhaps most difficult challenge is a direct result of the euro crisis itself. As discussed earlier, a large part of the policy response has been to move towards deeper political integration in the euro zone. The fiscal compact, the European semester, the two-pack, the six-pack and the rest add up to far more intrusive monitoring of national governments' fiscal and economic policies. The Commission now has the responsibility to vet and, if need be, propose changes to national governments' budgets even before their parliaments have seen them. Coming on top of the loss of monetary and exchange-rate policy due to the introduction of the euro, the result is a significant transfer of power from national to European level.

It should not be a surprise that one consequence is a crisis of democratic accountability. As a senior German finance ministry official put it to Ulrike Guérot and Thomas Klau of the European

Council on Foreign Relations in 2012, "the weakness of the system is not about spending and how to promote growth, but about legitimacy".[3] Some of those who pushed for a single currency at and before Maastricht always thought it would take closer political union for it to work satisfactorily – indeed, a few pressed for EMU precisely because they thought it would force the creation of a United States of Europe. But most voters and most governments were not persuaded. Now a form of political union is indeed being brought in, not, however, as a positive result of careful national debate and as a consequence of economic success, but rather as a negative outcome to ward off economic failure. That surely will make it even harder to persuade voters to support the entire notion of political union.

It does not help that in parts of Europe democracy is going through something of a crisis at home. There are many manifestations of this. One was the fact that both Greece and Italy had technocratic prime ministers thrust on them during the euro crisis. Greeks have long been fed up with their political leaders. In Italy, voters have become increasingly disillusioned with their entire political class, often known as *La Casta* and widely reviled for its excessive cost and many privileges. Yet neither country was happy to have unelected leaders appointed in place of elected ones. It was this, perhaps more than a lost love for Europe, that led so many Greeks to vote for fringe parties in May 2012 and so many Italians to back Grillo's Five Star movement in February 2013. In eastern Europe, Bulgarians have spent most of the past two years protesting in the streets against their government. Romanians seem equally fed up with a long-running feud between their president and their prime minister.

Hungary deserves a special mention here, as it has run into much condemnation in Brussels. Viktor Orban's centre-right Fidesz party won a smashing electoral victory in 2010 after the outgoing Socialist government became discredited. But Orban proceeded to rewrite the constitution in ways that cemented Fidesz's dominance over Hungary's institutions and its intimidating control of the country's media. Although the EU has managed to get the government to rewrite provisions impinging on central-bank and judicial independence, it has found its leverage over the government worryingly limited. As was discovered as long ago as 2000, when the EU tried to freeze relations with an Austrian government that included the far-right Jörg Haider as a coalition partner, a country that is a full member is much less susceptible to outside pressure than an applicant. Moreover, Orban's membership of the centre-right European People's Party transnational group is often said to have restrained his fellow heads of government from being too harsh on him. The result has been to damage the cause of liberal democracy in its broadest sense.[4]

Now the challenge from the euro crisis threatens to make matters worse. Indeed, in their first encounter with the European semester, several national leaders, even those normally thought of as pro-European, went out of their way to criticise the Commission for its intrusiveness. Spain's Mariano Rajoy announced in 2012 that it was for his government, not the Commission, to decide the right level of the Spanish budget deficit. In France, Hollande early on declared that, while the Commission was within its rights to demand pension reform, his government should be left to decide what sort of changes to make and how quickly to make them. The Italian government rejected a criticism of its longer-term debt sustainability. And when Belgium, the most pro-European country of all, was rebuked over its budget deficit, one Belgian government minister asked aloud: "Who is Olli Rehn?" (the economic-affairs commissioner).[5]

Yet it is too simple to see the problem as merely one of excessive Commission interference in matters better left to elected national governments. That was to some extent true when it came to the operation of the stability and growth pact. When Gerhard Schröder and Jacques Chirac came together in 2003 to overturn any suggestion of Commission-imposed sanctions on their two countries for breaching the terms of the pact, they were simply asserting greater legitimacy for elected political leaders. There was little in the way of broader economic fallout. Indeed, that is precisely why their colleagues, with the partial exception of the rule-loving Dutch, made so little fuss about the demise of the pact at the time.[6]

But the euro crisis has changed this completely, by bringing into the picture nationally sanctioned rescue funds. A bail-out of an excessively indebted country has to be approved by national authorities, including national parliaments, because ultimately it must rest on the credit of sovereigns. As became clear in May 2010, the EU budget is too small for this purpose. For such a fund to attract its AAA rating, it requires guarantees from creditworthy governments. And in national democracies, that needs the backing of national parliaments. This is one reason the issue of democratic accountability in Europe has become so acute. When it is clear that something has to be decided at European level, the EU treaties have a supranational, if not always satisfactory, mechanism of accountability. When decisions are wholly national, similarly, a national system should work. But in the euro crisis decisions are, in effect, hybrid: they are taken at a European level, but the funds being committed are provided nationally. In such cases issues of accountability and democratic control can all too easily fall through the cracks.

Hence the experience of the Finnish parliament (Eduskunta), which has repeatedly demanded specific collateral for loans to Greece and others. And hence also the growing role of the German Bundestag in demanding the right to approve every bail-out individually. The Bundestag's demand for a say in bail-outs is strongly supported by another crucial German institution, the Bundesverfassungsgericht, or constitutional court, based in Karlsruhe. The constitutional court has played a big role in the euro crisis, chiefly because a number of plaintiffs have repeatedly petitioned it to declare various decisions to be unconstitutional because they infringe the German basic law – ranging from the first Greek bail-out to the establishment of the European Stability Mechanism to the ECB's programme of outright monetary transactions (OMT) to support sovereign-bond markets. So far the court has not ruled against anything, but it has often hedged its verdicts with language suggesting that there are limits to how far the federal government in Berlin can go. In the case of OMT, it made its disapproval clear but transferred the case to the European Court for a ruling. It has also made clear, including in its ruling on the Lisbon treaty, that it does not see the European Union's democratic credentials as sufficiently strong.[7]

Many Euro-enthusiasts are horrified both by the Karlsruhe court and by the Bundestag's assertion of control over bail-out decisions. They see a creeping renationalisation at work, all of a piece with Merkel's new-found enthusiasm for inter-governmentalism and the "union method" at the expense of the traditional community method.

Germany's lack of enthusiasm for the EU institutions, notably the Commission but also the European Parliament, which used always to attract strong German support, is to them part of the same pattern. What such enthusiasts tend to favour instead as a way to inject more democratic accountability into EU-related decisions is to give a much greater role to the only directly elected EU institution: the Parliament in Strasbourg. Yet this runs into huge problems of its own.

Strasbourg blues

The Parliament is certainly ready and eager to step forward. It has already played a constructive role in drawing up the necessary legislation for the European semester. It wants to do more in the way of scrutiny of the Commission's decisions and of any contracts for reform that national governments might accept. Yet the notion that it can help to fill the gap in the euro zone's democratic accountability and in providing greater legitimacy for the system to ordinary voters is far-fetched and may be highly dangerous, for four reasons.

The first is institutional. The Parliament is quintessentially a body that brings together representatives from all 28 EU countries. It was relatively easy for the Council of Ministers to establish a sub-formation in the Eurogroup and now the Eurogroup summit. It is also fairly simple to form a tacit understanding that the economics commissioner as well as the Commission president should, like the presidents of the ECB and of the European Council, come from a euro-zone country. It is much harder to do the same in the Parliament. Indeed, the chair of the economic and monetary affairs committee during most of the euro crisis has been Sharon Bowles, a British Liberal Democrat. Some have muttered about this, and a few enthusiasts, including the French Eiffel group, have even suggested setting up a separate or "inner" euro-zone parliament. But to most this would excessively institutionalise the already worrying divide between euro ins and euro outs.

A second objection is that the Parliament itself lacks legitimacy. It has been directly elected for the past 44 years, yet the turnout in successive elections has steadily fallen. European elections everywhere are treated as essentially national polls, in which voters typically register protests against their governments or back populist parties. There is no sense among voters of any Europe-wide political parties: few have heard of the main political groups or have any clue about what they actually stand for. The results of European elections are not seen to translate in any way into changes of executive power within the EU; they do not even determine the presidency of the Parliament, since this is divided between the two biggest groups for the term of each legislature. Few people have any idea what the Parliament does or who their MEP is. In short, for most ordinary Europeans the Parliament seems to be part of the problem of remote and largely unaccountable EU institutions, and not part of the solution.

Various remedies have been suggested for these ills. One old favourite is to give the Parliament more powers, which has been done so much that for most purposes it has become a co-equal legislator with the Council of Ministers. The idea is that if the Parliament is seen to be exercising fuller powers in the EU, voters will take it more seriously. And indeed the Parliament, especially through its committees, has become an important and at times extremely valuable part of the legislative process, often improving directives and regulations more effectively than the Council. Many people cite the examples of the REACH chemicals rules and the services directive, which was in part resurrected by the Parliament, as examples.

Yet even Europhiles remain dissatisfied with the Parliament. A believer in democracy might expect the three biggest groups, the centre-right European People's Party (EPP), the centre-left Progressive Alliance of Socialists and Democrats (S&D) and the centrist Alliance of Liberals and Democrats for Europe (ALDE), to debate from their different political standpoints and vote accordingly, as happens in national parliaments. But far more often the big groups come together to make the Parliament more of a lobby or non-governmental organisation that sets itself up against the Commission and the Council of Ministers, rather than acting like a normal legislature. The Parliament is fond of passing largely meaningless foreign-policy resolutions. Unlike most national parliaments, it always wants both more powers for itself and a bigger budget – something few of its voters would support. The divide between voters and their MEPs was made starkly clear when the Dutch and French overwhelmingly rejected the constitutional treaty, which had been approved by almost all the MEPs from those countries.

Another suggestion has been to give the Parliament a bigger and more explicit role in choosing the Commission, especially its president. The Lisbon treaty provides that the European Council, taking account of the results of the European elections, should nominate a candidate, who is then "elected" by an absolute majority of the Parliament. (The Parliament is also required to approve the entire college of commissioners, but not each individual, this time by simple majority.) Most of the political groups have taken this language as an excuse to put forward their preferred candidate for the Commission presidency before the European elections. The S&D group, for instance, has proposed the current president of the Parliament, Martin Schulz; the ALDE has put forward its leader, Guy Verhofstadt; and the EPP is proposing Jean-Claude Juncker. The idea is that this should make the elections matter more to voters, since they will, in effect, be indirectly choosing the next Commission president.

Yet this solution to the democratic deficit is unlikely to help. Most ordinary people remain profoundly ignorant both of the political groups that are proposing candidates and of the candidates themselves: it is hard to see British Labour voters, say, turning out in large numbers because they are enthused about the prospect of Schulz as the Commission president. Worse, by making the Commission more beholden to the Parliament than it already is, the plan would upset the EU's institutional structure. Unlike the Parliament, the Council of Ministers cannot sack the Commission; if the Parliament has the decisive voice in the Commission presidency, this would aggravate the imbalance, making it all the more likely that the Commission and Parliament would come together to act against national governments. And worst of all, the plan would sharply reduce the field of candidates to become president of the Commission: no incumbent government leader would be ready to step down to campaign as part of the European elections.[8]

Besides the European Parliament's own failings as an institution that can fill the EU's and the euro zone's democratic deficits, there is a third reason to doubt that it will be the answer. This is that an increasing number of populists and extremists are now represented in the Parliament. On one level, this could be seen as positive: at least this strand of opinion, often hostile to both the EU and the euro, will be fully represented in the European institutions. But the presence of such a destructive group of oddballs, loonies and closet racists is hardly likely to enhance the reputation of the Parliament or make it easier for it to play a role in holding the EU's policymakers to account.

And there is yet another, fourth reason, why the Parliament will never be the answer to legitimacy and democracy in the euro zone. This is that decisions over euro-zone bail-outs, the rescue of European banks or fiscal transfers to troubled countries will always involve national taxpayers' money. The Bundestag's insistence on approving such measures is not mainly a symptom of a sudden Euroscepticism in Germany. It is something far simpler: the notion that, where national taxpayers' money (or credit) is being used, there must be some national control over what it is being used for – and also some national accountability. There is no way in which a European-level body could supply either of these, least of all one whose *raison d'être* is always to increase its powers and to spend more.

Back to national democracy

This points to another answer to Europe's democratic deficit: greater national involvement. The spread of national referendums on European issues is part of this: besides the two habitual practitioners, Denmark and Ireland, several other countries now put substantial new EU treaties or decisions such as whether to join the euro to popular vote. France and Austria have, at various times, suggested that a decision to admit Turkey to the EU would have to be approved similarly (France put the issue of UK membership to a referendum in 1972, securing a large "yes" majority). Under its European Union Act, the UK is required to put any treaty involving a significant transfer of power to Brussels to a referendum. And David Cameron has promised that, if he is re-elected as prime minister in 2015, he will ask the British people to decide whether to remain in a reformed EU.

Referendums are, however, always chancy affairs. So it is really national parliaments that are best placed to improve democratic input and accountability in the EU and the euro zone. Their role in the

EU machinery has been increased by successive treaties. Since the Lisbon treaty, national parliaments have been given specific powers to police "subsidiarity", the provision that decisions should be taken at the lowest possible level. Under a yellow/orange-card procedure, national parliaments acting together can ask for Commission proposals for legislation to be withdrawn. The treaty also recognises COSAC, a co-ordinating body of European committees from national parliaments, most of which maintain offices in the European Parliament building in Brussels. There is increasing interest in the more effective forms of national scrutiny of European legislation, with the most popular models being Denmark and Finland, where parliamentary committees hold the government to account for decisions it takes in the Council of Ministers.

The euro crisis has put renewed emphasis on the role of national parliaments. The Bundestag, the Eduskunta, the Dutch Tweede Kammer and others have asserted a direct interest in approving any decisions that rely on their taxpayers' credit or money. And the new powers of the Commission to scrutinise draft national budgets, to issue recommendations to countries with excessive budget deficits or with large current-account deficits (or surpluses) are inevitably impinging on national parliamentary authority over public spending and taxation. For this reason it has become desirable, indeed essential, that the Commission should engage with national parliaments. So far, its response to the yellow-card procedure has been disappointing: only one proposal has been withdrawn, and the Commission disgracefully ignored a complaint from 18 different parliamentary chambers about the legal basis for a European public prosecutor. But as the system beds down, the Commission should end up doing more at the behest of national parliaments, and it must be expected that the commissioner for economic and monetary affairs and his or her officials will have to appear before them more often.

Yet even this might not be enough to lend greater democratic legitimacy to a far more intrusive system of economic control. That is why several analysts and commentators have at various times suggested much greater moves towards fuller political union, with an elected Commission that includes a finance minister, or at least an elected president of the Commission and, as a necessary adjunct, a substantial euro-zone budget. No doubt if the European project were to take a leap into full political union, some kind of federal election would become necessary. But at least for the foreseeable future, neither European voters, nor national governments, nor Europe's political leaders seem remotely ready for any such steps.[9]

10 How the euro spoilt any other business

IT WOULD BE EASY TO FORM THE IMPRESSION that, at least since late 2009, nothing much has happened in the European Union except for the euro crisis and its economic and financial repercussions. Yet the normal business of the European institutions in such areas as competition policy, policing the single market, agriculture, transport, social and employment regulation, and trade has perforce continued. The budget has continued to be spent and, especially in the negotiations for 2014–20, quarrelled over. The European Council has also, from time to time, been summoned to discuss matters other than the economy and the euro, even if it has quickly reverted to these more momentous issues. There has been less EU legislation than before, in part because governments have long made clear that they wanted less. Even so, overall it is undeniable that the euro crisis has spilt damagingly into many other areas of EU activity.

One example is climate change, an issue where the Europeans have for a long time prided themselves on being in the lead globally. The EU was a pioneer not just in signing the Kyoto protocol on carbon-dioxide emissions but also in setting up the world's first emissions-trading scheme (ETS). In 2008 it adopted a "20-20-20" strategy: setting 2020 as a target date by which all EU members undertook to cut greenhouse-gas emissions by 20%, to raise the share of renewables in energy consumption by 20% and to improve energy efficiency by 20%. Yet partly thanks to its economic woes, the EU's influence at the 2009 Copenhagen environment summit, and again at the 2013 Warsaw environment summit, was minimal. The ETS has largely been a failure, as too many permits were issued and too many industries exempted. Carbon prices under the scheme have dropped too low to make much difference.

Popular enthusiasm for curbing climate change has faded, even though, thanks to its recession, the EU as a whole will just about hit the 20-20-20 target. In part the feeling has grown that there is little point in pursuing this without further action by the United States and China. But loss of interest in climate change also reflects Europeans' preoccupation with the euro crisis and rising joblessness, creating a strong desire not to harm competitiveness with too many "green" taxes. As it is, European industries pay four times as much for gas and twice as much for electricity as their American rivals, which are benefiting from cheap shale gas. In its January 2014 proposals for new climate-change targets, the Commission suggested only that all EU members should aim to cut greenhouse-gas emissions by 40% by 2040; it dropped national targets for renewables, proposing only that the EU as a whole should push its share up to 27% on the same timescale.[1]

Energy policy more broadly has also suffered from neglect, in part because of the euro crisis. In 2009, shortly before it broke, the EU adopted a "third energy package" that envisaged a much tougher approach to liberalising gas and electricity markets, including separating production, transmission and supply (a process known as unbundling). Various regulations and directives to implement this package have since been adopted. And the Commission has also initiated competition proceedings against Gazprom, Russia's energy giant. The Russians have been lobbying hard for changes to the third energy package. But partly because Europe's economic woes raised new concerns about high energy costs, progress towards implementing unbundling has been slow or non-existent.

A similar story could be told in many other areas of EU business, ranging from transport to agricultural to industrial policy. Partly because the 28 commissioners all want to have something to do, there is no shortage of papers and draft proposals for legislation on the table. But the enthusiasm with which they are pursued and the attention paid to them by national governments, and especially by leaders in the European Council, has of necessity been limited by the need to focus on their more pressing concerns for the euro. In many cases this has mattered only a little. Indeed, less regulation in unnecessary places is now widely seen as a desirable and not a bad outcome. But in a few areas the lack of attention from the top has been positively damaging.

A prime example is efforts to strengthen and complete the single market. After the 2005 fiasco over the "Bolkestein" directive to open up services markets, named after the Dutch commissioner then in charge, which was demonised as a Frankenstein directive in the French referendum campaign on the EU constitution and linked to a supposed influx of Polish plumbers, the eventual text was much watered down, leaving a single market in services largely incomplete.[2] The digital economy is also not properly covered by single-market rules: price-comparison websites remain fiercely national, as do most consumer-protection laws, taxes, electronic-waste rules and postal systems. The result is that e-commerce, which has mushroomed in the United States and in several individual European countries, is notably undeveloped across European borders.

Yet over the past few years most talk of extending the single market, often promoted by liberal countries like the UK and Sweden, has been drowned out by fears associated with recession and rising unemployment. The fate of Mario Monti's 2010 report, *A New Strategy for the Single Market*, is particularly instructive.[3] The report was commissioned by José Manuel Barroso, the European Commission president, long before Monti became Italian prime minister, when he was thought of as just another former commissioner. In the report, Monti proposed further work to complete the single market in energy, digital and services, and also suggested ways to bolster the green economy and to improve free movement of people and capital (including some elements of tax harmonisation).

By a cruel irony, however, the report was published on the same day as the Greek bail-out was agreed. The European Council had earlier in the same year proposed a new EU 2020 strategy to follow from the earlier Lisbon strategy, which was meant to create the world's "most competitive and dynamic knowledge-based economy" by 2010. But, just as the Lisbon strategy had never really been implemented, partly because neither France nor Germany seemed to believe in it, so the EU 2020 strategy seems to have been quietly abandoned. The

European Council duly endorsed the Monti report, but little more was done to pursue it. Monti himself has gone further: he has warned that because of the euro crisis, repatriation of bank lending, different interest rates round Europe and rising protectionist pressures, there is a real risk that the single market could go through a period of "rollback and even disintegration".[4]

The price of inaction

One could run through almost any area of EU business in the past five years and reach similar conclusions. Normal activity has continued and there have even been some noteworthy policy successes, for example in reforming the common fisheries policy to end the practice of discarding catches. But time and again work has stalled as commissioners, officials and national ministers have been sidetracked into efforts to resolve the euro crisis. The single market remains incomplete, partly because the attention of the commissioner concerned, Michel Barnier, has been focused mainly on bank and financial regulation. Although almost all governments have called for less as well as better regulation, the Commission's sausage machine has continued to churn out unwanted rules. Trade policy has been active, with several free-trade deals negotiated or in the pipeline. But the involvement of EU leaders has been noticeable mainly by its absence.

The decision in 2013 to launch talks towards a Transatlantic Trade and Investment Partnership (TTIP) was driven in large part by the Europeans, who were mainly concerned not to lose out from Barack Obama's new focus on Asia. But the worry is that concerns about Europe's economies, high unemployment and the future of the single currency may well continue to divert political and media attention away from the important details in the TTIP. All trade talks run into trouble, with special interests sheltering such things as agriculture, audio-visual services, rules on public procurement, and food and veterinary standards. Already there are signs of emerging doubts about the TTIP's chances on the European side. On the American side, the US Congress has not even given Obama the trade promotion authority that he needs to pass a deal. The World Trade Organisation's

Doha round largely fell apart, with what was eventually enacted being more of a mouse than an elephant – though that was mainly because of objections from emerging countries like India, not because of the Europeans. There is every chance that the same could happen with the TTIP.

That would be a double missed opportunity, for as well as boosting economic growth, the TTIP could be the last chance that Europe and the United States will get to set standards and rules for world trade before a newly powerful China exerts its influence. And yet, even before the talks began, the French managed to block any discussion of their notorious cultural exception, under which protection of audio-visual products such as films is allowed despite free-trade rules. Transatlantic differences over telecoms, internet and bank regulation, and over the rules governing airlines and shipping, remain wide. Phytosanitary rules on the use of hormones in meat or for genetically modified crops are also potential stumbling blocks. With the euro continuing to divert everybody's attention, European elections and the choice of a new Commission approaching, and Obama still denied fast-track authority by Congress, the chances of a successful outcome to the TTIP talks do not look all that high.

A last area where the EU has managed less than it might have done over the past five years is justice and home affairs (JHA). Under the Lisbon treaty, most activity in JHA has moved from being done inter-governmentally and by unanimity to being carried out by the community method, and thus subject to qualified-majority voting and co-decision with the European Parliament. Viviane Reding, the justice commissioner, has produced a number of proposals, such as a revised European arrest warrant, a European public prosecutor's office, new extradition arrangements, and common immigration and asylum rules. Yet few of these have made much progress, not only because the UK, Denmark and Ireland have opt-outs (and the UK is opting out en bloc from all JHA rules in 2014), but also because of the general distraction of the euro crisis.[5]

The other reason JHA has proved disappointing is that immigration has suddenly become such a toxic issue in many countries. The rise of populist parties has been driven in many cases by increasing voter hostility to immigration, even within the EU. The belief that migrants from central and eastern Europe are taking jobs or claiming generous welfare benefits has become widespread. The British, Dutch and Germans are all talking of introducing new rules to stop "benefit tourism". Opinion pollsters have found that by far the biggest reason British voters give for backing the UK Independence Party is not its anti-EU policy but its anti-immigration one.

Some political leaders, including the UK's David Cameron, have questioned the principle of free movement of labour within the EU, on the grounds that when it was enshrined nobody expected the club to include such relatively low-income countries as Romania and Bulgaria. Cameron has suggested that any future enlargement to take in new countries might have to be accompanied by permanent controls on free movement of people – an irony given that the UK has traditionally been the strongest supporter of EU expansion to admit new members. The Swiss vote in February 2014 to put quotas on immigration even from within the EU was not just a breach of Switzerland's various agreements with the EU that could threaten the country's access to the single market; it was also a harbinger of similar thinking within the EU itself.

A Commission of neglect

The euro crisis has, in short, managed to distract attention from much of the rest of the agenda of the Commission, national governments and the European Parliament since 2009. Economic difficulties have inevitably sapped the European Union of much of its broader influence in the world. And because Europe's political leaders have spent so much time trying to repair the defects in their single currency, they have devoted much less attention to considering the future shape and direction of the EU. As the immediate worry that the euro might collapse dissipates and with the prospect of a new Commission and new European Parliament just ahead, Brussels is left with a European project that is itself in some danger of falling apart due to political neglect.

Some have suggested that a good place to start improving things might be with the Commission itself. In the UK and many northern countries, the notion that the Commission should be doing less but also doing it better is widely shared: even Barroso has expressed a similar wish. The Dutch and Germans have been especially vociferous in demanding less red tape and bureaucracy, and more attention to the principle of subsidiarity, which provides that action should be taken at European level only if it is more efficacious than acting at national level. But even across southern Europe, the feeling that sometimes the Commission and the European Parliament are too intrusive has spread.

One reason the Commission has traditionally found it hard to respond to calls for it to do less is that there are too many commissioners. There is a widespread consensus that 28 is too big a number for the college. Not surprisingly, each commissioner wants to make his or her mark with legislation. Worse, partly because the Commission does not act like a government, there is no real system for co-ordinating and prioritising its actions. Instead, the Commission operates in a silo-like way, with individual directorates operating largely without much reference to each other or to the president. The proposal in the constitutional treaty and then the Lisbon treaty that there should be fewer commissioners than one per country was quietly shelved as a gesture to secure Irish approval of the treaty the second time round. At least some governments would like to find a way to revive its spirit, perhaps by creating senior and junior commissioners.

11 Europe's place in the world

THE EUROPEAN UNION'S HOPES that the Lisbon treaty would enable it to play a bigger global political role to match its economic weight were dealt a cruel blow by the onset of the euro crisis. That the Greek problem surfaced just as EU leaders were about to pick a new foreign-policy boss was especially galling. Over the past few years EU foreign policy has suffered not just because the euro crisis has been a distraction, but also because it has eaten away at the respect that the rest of the world previously had for a Europe that had long been considered an economic giant but a political pygmy.

The Maastricht treaty in 1992, building on arrangements previously known as European Political Co-operation, established a European Common Foreign and Security Policy (CFSP) as what was then called the EU's "second pillar", to be operated initially on an inter-governmental basis. Successive treaties expanded the scope and role of the CFSP, which was later brought under the normal community rules, though always subject to unanimous not majority voting. The 2009 Lisbon treaty then created the post of high representative for foreign and security policy, to be in charge of a new European External Action Service (EEAS). This formalised a job that was previously occupied by Spain's Javier Solana, a former secretary-general of the North Atlantic Treaty Organisation (NATO).

Yet for all the aspirations of the treaties and despite the creation of new institutions, it has always been hard to secure the consent of member countries to a genuine common foreign policy. The main problem has been with the larger members, notably the UK and France, which continue to see themselves as having a global role of their own. Both are nuclear powers, as well as permanent members of the UN Security Council. The UK, in particular, has often frustrated hopes of the EU playing a bigger security or defence role, for instance blocking any suggestion of setting up an EU military headquarters. Although France under Sarkozy rejoined NATO's military structure and has embarked on direct military co-operation with the UK, it too has continued to aspire to a global role of its own, especially in Africa.

But it has often been almost as difficult to find unanimous agreement among other countries. Even as Maastricht was being negotiated and ratified, for example, the outbreak of war in the Balkans provided a first big test that Europe largely failed. It was the Germans who insisted in 1991 on the early recognition of Croatia, followed by other ex-Yugoslavian states; and it was Jacques Poos, the foreign minister of Luxembourg, who proclaimed this to be "the hour of Europe".[1] Yet subsequently the Europeans could not agree on whether or when to intervene in their own backyard, and it took the Americans to knock heads together and secure the Dayton agreement in 1995 that stopped most of the fighting in Bosnia.

Although in subsequent years there were more successful efforts to find consensus within the EU on smaller foreign-policy issues, it has often proved impossible on larger ones. There have been big differences among the larger EU countries on policy towards Russia, for instance, which the Russians under Vladimir Putin have gleefully exploited. And, as the Balkans showed, when it comes to war, the Europeans have more often been divided than united. Most obviously, the EU split over Iraq in 2003, with Germany and France joining Russia in opposing the war, while the UK, Italy, Spain and several countries from eastern Europe supported it (this was the time when the American defence secretary, Donald Rumsfeld, spoke of there being a new and an old Europe). A more recent example of division came over the 2011 war in Libya, which was prosecuted vigorously by the UK and France but opposed by Germany.

Foreign policy blues

The EU's aspirations to build a stronger and more cohesive foreign policy to increase its influence in the world were never likely to be all that successful. But they have taken a further knock because of the euro crisis. By an unfortunate coincidence, the choice of the first new high representative came at the same time. The bargaining over names for jobs was, as usual, a shambles, with the UK's prime minister, Gordon Brown, first trying to push David Miliband, the foreign secretary, into the job. In the end Miliband rejected it and the post went instead to the little-known Catherine Ashton, a former trade commissioner whose previous public-policy life was limited to running a health authority and serving in the UK's House of Lords, and who had limited knowledge of or experience in foreign affairs.

Predictably, the establishment of the new EEAS and the experiment with Ashton as a more powerful EU high representative have both been disappointing. Apart from her own limitations, the job has become almost too big for one person to do. As well as being high representative, she is a vice-president of the Commission, she chairs the Foreign Affairs Council and she is a guardian of British interests in Brussels. She was not given any deputies, even though the exigencies of the job often require her to be in two places at once. Everything has taken longer than expected and Ashton has continued to be overshadowed not just by national foreign ministers but also by José Manuel Barroso, president of the European Commission, and Herman Van Rompuy, the first permanent president of the European Council. The CFSP was supposed to sharpen the way the EU represented itself in the world, but the results have frequently seemed to do the opposite: both presidents as well as Ashton attend bilateral summits with the Americans, Russians and Chinese, for example. And the EU has continued to field too many assorted leaders at G8 and G20 summit meetings.

Even so, over the past year, Ashton has recorded some notable successes. These include a groundbreaking deal between Serbia and Kosovo that has enabled the first to open membership negotiations and the second to be given a membership perspective, ahead of Bosnia. Ashton has also been a key member of the team negotiating a tentative nuclear deal with Iran, which was in part her own personal achievement. She has become an indispensable partner of successive American secretaries of state, first Hillary Clinton and later John Kerry, with whom she has far more contact than most European foreign ministers ever do. She was the only diplomatic leader to meet the deposed Egyptian president, Muhammad Morsi, after his imprisonment. And she has played a leading role in negotiations to end the war in Syria. Yet despite all these achievements, the overall record of the EU in foreign policy has not been a strong one – and part of the reason for this has been the EU's poor economic performance and the distraction of the euro crisis, which has reduced Europe's overall influence.[2]

A further consequence of that crisis has been that defence budgets across Europe, already strained, have been further cut. In 2009 a European Council summit agreed to step up Europe's military ambitions, with some talk of being able to deploy 60,000 troops within 60 days. But five years on little has come of this. The EU is meant to have two 1,500-strong battlegroups available at short notice, but none has ever been used. Overall, EU countries spend less than 1.5% of GDP on defence, far below both the agreed NATO target of 2% and the 4%-plus spent by the United States. Defence spending has shrunk as a share of public spending. And the money is not spent as effectively as it could be were there to be more collaboration across borders.[3] Successive American defence secretaries have continued to voice frustration as Europe has become in their eyes more of a consumer than a provider of security, a growing problem as the Americans pivot their attention towards Asia.

The experience with the onset of the Arab spring in January 2011, which coincided with one of the worst moments of the euro crisis, was illuminating. The Europeans, like the Americans, were taken by surprise by the sudden upsurge of people power, first in Tunisia and then in Egypt. The subsequent decision to intervene in Libya to stop a possible massacre in Benghazi by troops loyal to Muammar Qaddafi was taken by the British and French governments, with the Germans against (indeed, Germany chose to abstain in the vote in the UN Security Council, of which it was a temporary member). But after only a few days the two biggest European military powers were forced to call for more American help, including the provision of drones, air-to-air refuelling and stocks of smart bombs.[4] Later, EU members were divided over whether and how to intervene in Syria, with the UK and France showing most interest in arming the rebels against the Assad regime, but Germany and others being broadly against (though the

August 2013 vote of the UK House of Commons against intervention in Syria has curbed British enthusiasm for any military adventures).

In economic terms, the EU has also shown itself unable always to work out the most sensible response to the Arab spring. Grand talk by the Commission and the EEAS of the three Ms – money, markets and migration – has all too often run into the sand. Partly because of the euro crisis, there was never much on offer to support a policy that became known as "more for more": the more Arab countries democratised, the more the EU would help them. Money was short. Fuller market access, particularly for agricultural products, has also been notable largely by its absence: three years after the Arab spring began, only Morocco has even begun negotiations on a deep free-trade deal with the EU.

As for migration, hostility towards it has grown as the euro crisis has led to rising unemployment, especially in the southern Mediterranean countries. Far from providing more routes to legal migration, ever more resources have been poured into tightening controls on illegal immigration. Leaky boats carrying would-be immigrants continue to sink in the Mediterranean around the Italian island of Lampedusa, one of the nearest parts of the EU to north Africa. Over migration, indeed, the EU now stands towards north Africa rather as the United States stands towards Mexico – and a part of the reason for this is the dire economic consequences of the euro crisis in terms of jobs and growth at home.

Eastern questions

The EU's relationship with countries to its east has also become more problematic in the past few years. One reason for this is that the traditional policy of enlargement to admit new countries has run into trouble. Enlargement has often been described as the EU's most successful foreign policy. In the 1980s, taking in countries like Greece, Spain and Portugal was hugely important in securing their transition from military dictatorship to democratic government. Even more spectacular was the process after the collapse of the Soviet Union of letting most of the central and eastern European countries that had formerly been under its sway into the European club. The transition of these countries to free-market economies and liberal democracy would have been far messier and might not have happened in all cases had it not been for the powerful lure of eventual EU membership. The contrast between Europe's success with transforming its eastern neighbours and the United States' failure with its southern neighbours is telling.

Since the admission of Bulgaria and Romania in 2007, however, the entire policy of enlargement has been under some threat. Part of the problem has been a growing disillusionment with past expansions of the EU. It is widely thought that Romania and Bulgaria were taken in as members before they were really ready; some of their present difficulties with a corrupt judiciary and political class could have been predicted in advance. Equally, Cyprus was allowed to join in 2004 even though the island's division between a Greek-Cypriot south and a Turkish-Cypriot north remained unsolved. Both the continuing Cyprus problem and Hungary's precarious democracy have reminded the EU that the leverage it has over its members is far less potent than its leverage over applicants. And for much of public opinion in Europe, enlargement has become fatally linked to newly unpopular immigration, especially from Bulgaria and Romania following the lifting of remaining controls on free movement of labour on January 1st 2014.

Despite all this, the Commission argues forcefully that the enlargement process is continuing. Croatia was admitted as the EU's 28th member in July 2013, and membership talks continue with Turkey and Montenegro (though talks with Iceland have been suspended). It is clear that the other western Balkan countries will eventually join the EU, if only because they have nowhere else to go. Indeed, it is only this prospect that has secured peace and stability in the region. Without the lure of EU membership, it would undoubtedly have been impossible to broker the 2013 deal between Serbia and its breakaway former province of Kosovo. Yet the reality is that the euro crisis, the broader malaise across the EU and increasing public hostility to unlimited immigration have combined to cast a pall over future enlargement.[5]

Who lost Turkey ... and Ukraine?

This is seen most clearly in relation to the EU's two biggest eastern neighbours, Turkey and Ukraine. After years of prevarication, including a negative Commission opinion on its membership application in 1987, it was seen as a triumph for both sides when at long last Turkey's application was accepted in 2004 and membership negotiations were formally opened in October 2005. The Turkish government, led by Recep Tayyip Erdogan, was eagerly pushing through big economic, social and political reforms to prepare the country for EU membership. Although substantial opposition persisted, especially in France, Germany and Austria, and although a disunited Cyprus remained a large obstacle, there was a genuine optimism that, maybe after another decade or so, Turkey might actually join the European club.

Yet eight years on few people even pretend that the talks with Turkey are going anywhere. Half of the 33 chapters of the negotiations remain frozen, either by Cyprus, or by France or by the EU as a whole, because Turkey has not implemented the Ankara protocol requiring it to open its ports and airports to Greek-Cypriot vessels. Only one chapter has been closed; and, in the past two years, only one has been opened. Several EU countries have made clear that, partly in response to their current economic difficulties, they are much less prepared to take the gamble of letting Turkey in. European leaders, distracted by the euro crisis, have barely engaged with the issue of their relations with Turkey, which have soured spectacularly. Understandably, many Turks seem to have lost interest in an EU that they believe has rejected them, perhaps out of anti-Muslim prejudice. And the EU has in turn lost much of the old leverage it had to encourage further reform in Turkey, which has drifted under Erdogan in an authoritarian direction, especially since the Gezi Park protests of June 2013 and the corruption scandal that broke in December 2013. Erdogan's attempt to rekindle the membership talks by visiting Brussels and Berlin in early 2014 and helping to revive talks on a Cyprus settlement have not done enough to repair Turkey's damaged image in Europe. Recent stories of corruption in the ruling party, and the country's growing economic difficulties, are creating renewed worries about Turkey's suitability as an EU aspirant.[6]

A similarly sad story can be told for the six countries of the EU's eastern partnership: Armenia, Azerbaijan, Belarus, Georgia, Moldova and Ukraine. After the Rose and Orange revolutions in Georgia and Ukraine, followed by Russia's war with Georgia in 2008, it looked as if, despite the Russian blockage on further expanding NATO, the Commission would at least be able to hold out a long-term prospect of EU membership to these countries. Yet once again European leaders took their eyes off the ball, partly because of the distraction of the euro crisis. At the Vilnius summit in November 2013, several countries, the biggest and most important of which was Ukraine, were meant to sign association agreements with the EU that could, eventually, have become a basis for possible membership. Instead, Russian pressure on Ukraine and some other countries to lean eastward paid off. Only the relatively small Georgia and Moldova were persuaded to stick to their European ambitions.

The sight of thousands of protesters on the streets and squares of a snowy Kiev, all waving EU flags to show their displeasure with the decision of their thuggish president, Viktor Yanukovych, to reject the EU association agreement in favour of closer links with Russia, was inspiring but also depressing. It was inspiring, because it showed how strong the appeal of ties with the EU still is to countries from the former Soviet block. But it was also depressing because, at least in part due to their own economic and political problems, EU leaders had paid too little attention to the admittedly dispiriting internal politics of Ukraine, allowing Russia quietly and insidiously to regain influence. Russia's president, Vladimir Putin, was able to derail Ukrainian plans to move towards Europe by the simple expedient of offering a no-strings-attached loan and a sharp cut in the gas price, which the EU simply could not match.[7]

That Ukraine subsequently grabbed the whole world's attention, especially during the 2014 Sochi winter Olympics, was more to do with its own dysfunctional politics and the bravery of its protesters than with the EU. The Americans woke up to the situation, and especially to the interference of Putin, earlier than the Europeans; a truth that became starker when a leaked recording, presumably made by Russian security services, showed Victoria Nuland, the assistant secretary for Europe in the State Department, saying to her ambassador in Kiev: "Fuck the EU." When a few days later Yanukovych's goons began to kill people in Kiev and elsewhere, matters rapidly spun out of his control. Soon enough he had been chased out of the capital and a new government was installed that may yet turn back towards the EU. But determined not to lose Ukraine, Putin promptly launched an invasion of Crimea. In mid-March 2014 Crimea, under the gaze of occupying Russian troops, declared its independence from Ukraine and asked to join the Russian Federation instead. The EU and the United States responded with a visa freeze and other sanctions on named individuals, as Russian forces gathered threateningly on the border with eastern Ukraine. The eventual outcome in Ukraine remains highly uncertain. But what seems clear is that the EU (and the West) drifted into its biggest confrontation with Russia since the cold war in part as an accidental by-product of its eastern neighbourhood policy, which distracted political leaders had left largely in the hands of Commission officials.

The EU's hopes of playing a bigger role in the world and in its neighbourhood were always going to be hard to realise. A declining share of the world's population and GDP, the rise of countries like Brazil, China and India and a diminishing appetite for military intervention have inevitably taken their toll. Yet the EU is still the world's biggest economy and single trading block. Had the crisis not sapped its economic power and its political will, it surely would have been able to exert a bigger foreign-policy influence than it has managed over the past five years, especially in its own neighbourhood. In short, the baleful effects of the euro crisis have been seen not just at home, but also in the EU's fading global clout.

SO WERE THE SCEPTICS RIGHT ALL ALONG? It is hard to avoid the conclusion that the single currency has been a terrible folly. Its failings have brought misery to many parts of Europe and gravely damaged the post-war European project. At the height of the financial crisis, in early 2009, Jean-Claude Trichet, president of the ECB, could plausibly argue: "In stormy seas, it's better to be on a large ship than in a small boat." But the euro turned out to be no mighty ocean liner; it was just a pleasure boat, good for showing off in sheltered waters but dangerous on the open seas, lacking bulkheads, lifeboats or even a trained skipper and crew.

Being locked in a single currency made it too easy, almost inevitable, for deficit countries to build up large imbalances in good times (pumped by the savings of surplus countries) and agonisingly difficult for them to adjust in hard times. William Hague, the UK's foreign secretary, was prescient when he predicted before the start of EMU (he was then the Conservative Party leader) that the currency zone would prove to be "a burning building with no exits". Or as Silvio Berlusconi, then Italy's prime minister, put it during the crisis, the euro is a "strange currency that does not convince anybody".

With national currencies bond markets would have been more alert, demanding higher interest rates long before weaker countries could build up such large external deficits. And when the crisis came, devaluation might have allowed them to regain competitiveness more easily. But this judgment has to be tempered. First, any gains from devaluation might have been frittered away though inflation; and inflation would have pushed up borrowing costs. Second, it is likely that Europe's currencies would have been linked in some way, and that the system would have been ripped apart when the financial storm blew in, with the Deutschmark appreciating sharply, the Italian lira devaluing and the French franc torn between the two. Third, currency chaos might easily have led to a protectionist free-for-all, undermining the single market.

In one form or another, major turmoil was probably unavoidable in Europe. What might once have been a currency crisis became, with the euro, a debt crisis. The euro allowed countries accustomed to high inflation to avoid reform in the good years as they benefited from low interest rates. Brutally, no doubt, the hardest-hit economies have been forced into overdue reforms, for instance in Ireland and Spain. Nowadays it is Italy and France, less traumatised but also less reformed than other countries, which present some of the biggest dangers to the future of the euro. They are too big to fail, too big to save and too big to bully from Brussels.

Europe's real folly was not to look for the gains from a single currency in terms of trade, financial integration, exchange-rate stability and economic efficiency, even if they might have been overstated. The madness was to believe that these benefits could be obtained on the cheap, without the political constraints, economic flexibility, financial transfers and risk-sharing mechanisms of genuine federations. What stands behind the euro? Germany? Up to a point. The ECB? Only sort of.

Almost everybody knew that the euro was incomplete when it was launched in 1999. Those who spoke up about the flaws were largely ignored. Those who kept quiet hoped that the problems would be repaired as and when they appeared. It was not an unreasonable assumption. The European project has always advanced through half-steps, in the knowledge that inadequacies would eventually require further half-steps to be made good. As Jean Monnet, a founding father, once put it: "Europe will be built through crises." The problem is that, when the euro crisis struck, it turned out to be far bigger than anyone had imagined. The debtors screamed for help, but the creditors feared being pulled under.

Yet the doomsayers were wrong in one crucial respect: they underestimated EU leaders' commitment to the European project. The euro has somehow survived, and many a short-seller has lost money betting on its demise. The euro's failings have been compensated by sheer political will and the fear of what might happen if it broke apart. Angela Merkel, the German chancellor, has staked hundreds of billions of euros-worth of German taxpayers' money to rescue other countries, while keeping her voters' trust. She held back those who wanted to push out Greece. The Greeks underwent appalling hardships to stay in. Cyprus did not walk out even after its banks were crushed. The ECB stretched its mandate to make sure that the euro would not break apart. And countries are still lining up to join: Latvia has just done so, Lithuania may follow in 2015.

So in the end, it was those who subscribed to the "coronation" theory of the single currency who were closest to the correct answer: monetary union should have been the culmination of political union, not the means to achieve it. Does that mean it is time to break up the misbegotten euro, just as countries abandoned the gold standard in the 1930s?

Redenomination would be acutely painful. Changing currency is different from leaving a fixed peg. Whether done by returning to national money, or by creating a Germanic northern euro and a Latin southern one, redenomination would mean that currencies, assets and liabilities would all be repriced abruptly. Some companies, in both creditor and debtor countries, would go bust. Some countries that devalued would be crushed by their euro-denominated debt and default. And there could be bank runs as depositors in southern countries rushed to move their savings to northern ones. The dislocation would be most acute for the deficit countries. If the euro has to be split, it would probably be least disruptive if Germany were to leave, either alone or with a group of northern neighbours, allowing the rest to devalue. But Germany would not avoid economic pain, and a euro without the EU's largest economy would make little sense.

It is also unlikely that the EU's single market would survive the implosion, as it would probably be followed by capital controls, trade barriers and, possibly, a wave of migration. Without the euro or the single market, the EU would become irrelevant. And vulnerable democracies in eastern Europe, and even in the south, could lose their political anchors. The tow-line that is pulling the Balkan countries towards the EU could snap. In short, it must still be better to refit the euro than to scrap it; and better still to do it during the current lull rather than wait for the next storm.

The measure of failure

The euro zone has undergone extensive patching. It now has a permanent rescue fund; tougher rules to monitor budgets and economic imbalances, with the threat of semi-automatic sanctions; and national balanced-budget rules through the fiscal compact. In principle, all recognise the need for structural reform to regain competitiveness and enhance growth. In September 2013, Wolfgang Schäuble, the German finance minister, boasted that the slow return to growth in the euro zone, and the rebalancing of current accounts in deficit countries, was proof that the much-criticised medicine was working:[1]

> *Systems adapt, downturns bottom out, trends turn. In other words, what is broken can be repaired. Europe today is the proof.*

Yet this is to miss the point. The euro's is a story of survival, not of success. Although it is limping back to growth, its weaker members

FIG 12.1 **The cost of failure**
Euro zone and US GDP at constant prices, 2007–14, 2007 = 100

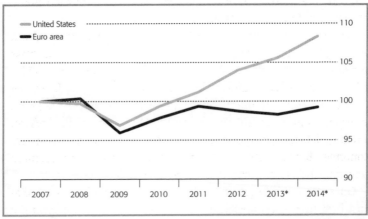

*Forecast
Source: IMF World Economic Outlook database, autumn 2013

have sunk deeper into debt. Mass unemployment and debt deflation in Greece are hardly evidence of successful adjustment. The question is not whether economies eventually bottom out, but whether politicians limit or worsen the damage. One answer is to compare the euro zone's performance with that of the United States (see Figure 12.1). European leaders like to blame the United States for their crisis, and to boast that aggregate public debts and budget deficits are healthier than those of the United States. So why is the United States doing so much better than the euro zone? US output has surpassed its pre-crisis peak and is growing moderately; the euro zone has yet to make up the lost ground and growth is still fragile. Unemployment was above 9% on both sides of the Atlantic in 2009, but it has since fallen close to 7% in the United States and risen above 12% in the euro zone. In the periphery the numbers are much worse. Europe as a whole has a less favourable demographic profile than the United States, so in terms of GDP per head the growth figures are a bit less dire. Nevertheless, the differences in performance are glaring.

A catalogue of errors

Europe's response has been slow, partial and often baffling to outsiders. The adjustment has been needlessly painful for the debtors, and probably needlessly expensive for the creditors. Leaders of the euro zone are unlikely to acknowledge their errors, but their many changes of policy amount to an implicit admission of them.

Who is to blame for the fiasco? Those who created such a death trap of a currency union, to begin with, followed by the reckless borrowers and the irresponsible lenders of the first decade of EMU. The rulers of deficit countries foolishly thought they could live in a Germanic currency union, and enjoy low interest rates, without becoming more Germanic in their attitude to budgets and wages. Certainly, deficits in the periphery were mirrored by surpluses in core economies. But the truth is that running large external deficits is more dangerous than having surpluses when a crisis hits.

Once the crisis began, though, it is the creditor countries that must bear prime responsibility. They were best placed to limit the fallout, because everybody needed their money, but they made it worse. Above all this means looking at the role played by Germany.

It is wrong to accuse it of selfishness or, worse, of trying to dominate Europe. Germany has undoubtedly staked much of its treasure (as have other countries) on saving the euro zone. But it made serious errors. It treated the crisis for far too long as a question of fiscal profligacy, and of individual countries. Mario Monti would quip that for Germany "economics is a branch of moral philosophy". Fiscal sinners had to atone, and the rightful had nothing to apologise for. Frequently in Germany economics was also a question of extreme legalism. Many of the most senior officials in the German finance ministry are lawyers, not economists, starting with Schäuble himself.

It was only in the summer of 2012 that Germany started to understand that the structure of the euro zone itself was unstable, and came around to accepting the need for a banking union. Even then it dragged its feet over anything that implied common liabilities, and insisted on a worryingly complex legal structure for the resolution mechanism.

The incoherence can be understood only in the light of Germany's twin terrors: the fear of moral hazard and the fear of collapse. These are best encapsulated by two dictums: "*chacun sa merde*", Nicolas Sarkozy's summary of Merkel's rejection of a joint bank rescue in 2008; and "*ultima ratio*", Merkel's justification for bailing out Greece in 2010. In other words, countries must deal with their problems on their own, and should be helped only as a last resort when the euro's survival is at stake. The constraints are meant to limit the liabilities of creditors and maintain pressure on debtors to reform. But they have raised the cost and length of the crisis, and allowed doubts about the euro's future to fester, thereby hampering the recovery in the periphery and accelerating financial fragmentation.

On the face of it, the heroes of the crisis are the two presidents of the ECB, Trichet and especially Mario Draghi, whose interventions kept the system going when the politicians were at each others' throats. The ECB gave timely warnings of the danger of imbalances, and responded decisively to the financial crisis. But once the trouble spread to sovereigns, it became much more cautious. It was willing to provide liquidity to banks, even those that were patently bust, but hesitated to do so overtly, even for solvent sovereigns. The Eurosystem of central banks cushioned the blow on deficit countries by accumulating large imbalances in the euro zone's payment settlement system, known as "Target II". At the height of the crisis in 2012, Germany's Bundesbank had, controversially, accumulated claims worth more than €750 billion against the ECB. So over and above the visible taxpayer-funded bail-out by the German government, economists argued bitterly over whether there was also a large stealthy bail-out via the Bundesbank. The Target II imbalance is perhaps best seen as a reflection of capital flight from the troubled periphery, and raises the question of whether central banks in creditor countries would have to take large losses should the euro break up and the debtor countries refuse to settle their Target II liabilities. In the event, the imbalance declined steadily after Draghi's "whatever it takes" speech in London in July 2012 restored confidence in the future of the euro zone.

That said, the ECB resisted for far too long the need to cut Greece's debt, and refused to let Ireland impose losses on bondholders. It devised an effective means of halting contagion only in the summer of 2012, after two years of crisis and half-hearted interventions in bond markets. If governments responded too late, the ECB often responded even later. It feared that if it acted too soon, governments would be only too happy to leave it alone to deal with the crisis. In the darkest days of the crisis, frustrated officials would tell Trichet: "You may end up being a central bank without a currency." To which he would reply: "And you may end up having a currency without a central bank."

The ECB had its own twin fears, both of them German. They were called "Bundesbank" and "Karlsruhe". The inflation-busting tradition of the Bundesbank meant that the ECB would rather flirt with deflation than let prices rise too high in Germany, or upset German savers by more aggressive lowering of interest rates. It never dared engage in the aggressive loosening of monetary policy, known as "quantitative easing" (involving the purchase of government bonds and other assets), long pursued by the US Federal Reserve and the Bank of England. Excessively low inflation, overly tight monetary policy and a high exchange rate made it even harder for the periphery to adjust relative to Germany. The Bundesbank openly opposed any resort to bond-buying to hold down borrowing costs. And the ECB soon ran up against the even greater intransigence of the German constitutional court, which ruled that Draghi's policy of outright monetary transactions (OMT), the one true firewall that had arrested the financial blaze, was illegal (though it offered a stay of execution by passing the case on to the European Court of Justice).

The fact that the crisis started in Greece, the clearest case of public spending gone wild and of a government unwilling or unable to enact reform, did much to reinforce the prejudices and fears of Germany and the ECB. It is plain to all in retrospect – and probably to those who knew the real numbers at the time – that the first Greek bail-out was ill-conceived. It treated Greece as a problem of liquidity rather than of solvency. The distinction is often hard to make, as it depends largely on a country's prospects for future growth and the interest rate that investors demand to hold its bonds. But Greece was plainly bankrupt. Its debt should have been cut early and decisively rather than late and messily, thereby giving private creditors the chance to dump Greek bonds.

Greece was pushed into panicked and excessive austerity – partly because its debt was so high, and partly because of a lack of credible tools to stabilise the euro zone. And when the programme failed, through a combination of Greece's shortcomings and those of its creditors, the threat of Grexit made everything much worse. The same was true, to a lesser extent, of other programme countries. The bail-outs were all too optimistic in their assumptions about the recessionary impact of austerity, and put too much faith in the notion that hairshirt economics would restore market confidence. The economies of Greece, Ireland and Portugal all performed worse than forecast: recessions were deeper and unemployment was higher. Perhaps most striking is the sharp worsening of debt-to-GDP ratios. This is only partly because deficits were increasing the debt, or the numerator. A bigger factor was that recession was shrinking output, or the denominator. The numbers for Greece were especially dire – its debt ratio reached 176% of GDP and joblessness passed 27% in 2013 (see Figures 12.2 and 12.3) – even though the one thing Greece did achieve was a reduction in the deficit more or less according to plan.

Countries in bail-out programmes were at first made to pay punitive rates of interest. It was only comparatively late that the focus

FIG 12.2 **The sins of the fathers ...**
Public debt, 1999–2014, % of GDP

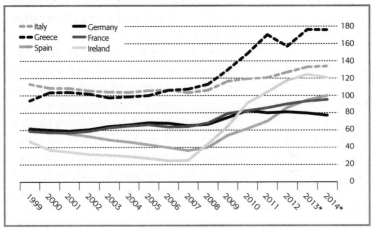

*Forecast
Sources: Eurostat; European Commission autumn forecast 2013

FIG 12.3 **... visited upon the sons?**
Unemployment rate, 1999–2014, %

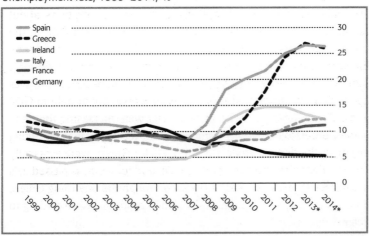

*Forecast
Sources: Eurostat; European Commission autumn forecast 2013

shifted from fiscal consolidation to structural reforms to make labour markets more flexible and enhance potential growth.

Of the members of the troika that negotiated the programmes, perhaps the biggest culprit is the European Commission. It had little experience of dealing with balance-of-payments crises and, under pressure from Germany, suffered from tunnel vision on fiscal rules.

Even so, the IMF cannot escape all blame. Its expertise was most needed at the start of the Greek programme, yet it had signed up to a deeply flawed programme. The IMF did, at least, try to redeem itself. Subsequent debt-sustainability assessments for Greece and Cyprus were more sober. It published a lessons-learnt report on Greece recognising that the country's debt should have been cut earlier.[2] IMF economists admitted that inappropriate fiscal multipliers had been used in forecasting the impact of austerity. And it has done much valuable future-oriented thinking, for instance on the design of a banking union and a putative future euro-zone budget. Such a spirit of self-examination and open inquiry has so far largely eluded the Commission.

Members of the European Parliament, who have started to inquire into the troika's workings, dream that it will be replaced one day by a fully fledged European Monetary Fund (built around the rescue fund, the European Stability Mechanism) that dispenses with the IMF. But it will be some time before the treaties can be changed to create such a body, and even longer for it to build up the necessary credibility.

It is tempting to argue that the euro-zone crisis would have been handled better if left entirely in the hands of the IMF. But given the size and interconnectedness of the euro zone's economies, and the slow pace of adjustment involved in "internal devaluation" with a fixed currency, the task was probably beyond the IMF's resources. It would probably always require substantial euro-zone funds to run such bail-out programmes.

Awkward co-operation between the Europeans and the IMF may therefore be needed for years to come. But the presence of the ECB in the troika is an anomaly. The central bank's mandate should not stretch to bargaining over budget cuts and reforms to labour markets, or threatening to cut off liquidity to banks if a country does not comply with its wishes. As the ECB becomes the euro zone's main bank supervisor, the conflict of interest is glaring. It is time, surely, for it to depart. One advantage is that the IMF, unshackled from the ECB, might be in a better position to push the central bank to loosen monetary policy.

To enumerate the errors of the troika is not to absolve Greece, and its Byzantine polity. It has proven obdurate when it comes to structural reforms. Nothing would have spared Greece the need for an agonising fiscal adjustment. But more coherence in the troika programme might have given Greece a greater chance of success, and avoided the death spiral that threatened to suck down the whole euro zone. Austerity was pursued too zealously, but given the levels of debt in the euro zone and the danger of losing access to markets in several countries, there was little space for anyone, apart from the likes of Germany, to engage in fiscal stimulus.

It is of course easier to be wise in retrospect. One explanation for the muddle was the real fear of financial instability. If Greece defaulted immediately, other countries might be pushed into bankruptcy too. Better to fudge the Greek numbers, buy time and wait for conditions to improve and growth to return. This argument would be stronger had the euro zone really used the time to redesign itself more profoundly. True, it cobbled together an inadequate bail-out fund. But it undid its own efforts with a ham-fisted bargain at Deauville and ignored the banking crisis for two years.

Perhaps the kindest thing that can be said is that the euro-zone's policymakers, confronted with their first major crisis, had to learn by trial and error. To borrow Churchill's apocryphal bon mot about Americans, the Germans can always be relied upon to do the right thing after they have exhausted all possible alternatives.

Hamilton and the F-word

The euro zone should look to the United States and ask itself: why does the prospect of default by one state not call into question the existence of the dollar? Why is the euro so flimsy that a default by Greece, accounting for less than 3% of the euro zone's GDP, should have been seen as an existential threat? The short answer is that the United States is a single federal country, while the euro zone is a much looser confederation of sovereign countries. It may use a single currency, but it has 18 national governments with 18 different economic policies.

The euro zone's financial system was sufficiently integrated to spread contagion, but not integrated enough to provide resilience. It has no central budget or other means of absorbing asymmetric shocks that hit one or two countries disproportionately. Until the ECB came up with the policy of OMT, it had no effective lender of last resort, so countries were in effect borrowing in a foreign currency. These faults meant that the no-bail-out rule, although enshrined in the Maastricht treaty, was not credible when the crisis hit. Yet the euro zone had no means of giving assistance to countries that got into trouble. By contrast, the US federal government has successfully resisted bailing out any of the states since the 1840s, leaving the markets to impose fiscal discipline.

Repeated bail-outs in the euro zone have, inevitably, led to more central controls on fiscal and economic policies. The "economic governance" created in recent years is a soup of incomprehensible jargon: six-pack, two-pack, fiscal compact, Euro Plus Pact, European semester, annual growth survey, excessive deficit procedure, macroeconomic imbalances procedure, "contractual arrangements" for reform, and much more. All this amounts to an unprecedented intrusion by an unaccountable EU bureaucracy that satisifes nobody: the Commission is accused by the debtors of doing the creditors' bidding, and by the creditors of being too soft on the sinners. This system is ultimately untenable. True, the IMF also imposes painful reforms when it is called in to help. But the IMF is a foreign doctor who eventually goes away. In the euro zone, the health inspectors move into the house forever.

In its weird hybrid construct, part United Nations and part United States, the euro zone often suffers from the worst features of both. Elected governments are being hollowed out by a loss of power to Brussels; but citizens have no direct say on decisions taken in Brussels. At some point the euro zone will discover something of the truths set out more than two centuries ago by Alexander Hamilton, the first American treasury secretary, in the federalist papers that he co-authored: trying to coerce sovereign states to follow common rules eventually leads to conflict. A federal system must thus act directly on the citizen, not the component states. Having created what is essentially a federal currency for Europe, the countries of the euro zone have much to learn from studying Hamilton, particularly the way he got the American federal government to assume the war debts of the former colonies and issue new national bonds backed by direct taxes. His new financial system helped transform the young republic from a basket case into an economic powerhouse.[3]

Bring back no bail-out

So what is the way forward? In the longer term, the only workable answer is surely to restore the credibility of the no-bail-out rule and allow countries to go bust if and when they get into trouble. The question is, can it be done under the Maastricht model of autonomous national economies, now modified by a handful of stricter centralised rules and a safety net based on *ultima ratio*? Or does it require more US-style fiscal federalism, involving the sharing of liabilities through autonomous central bodies? Put another way, should "solidarity" in the euro zone happen only in extremis, after a country gets into trouble, in the form of "mutual assurance" by governments offering help in return for tough conditions?[4] Or should it take place automatically, for instance raising European taxes to deal with banking risks or, say, unemployment insurance?

Expert opinion is divided. Ashoka Mody, a former senior IMF official, argues in a 2013 paper for Bruegel, a think-tank in Brussels, that European officials should recognise that the federalist impulse is at a standstill.[5] Germany and other surplus countries will not accept any mutualisation of risk, be it in the form of joint debt or joint liability for the banks. Instead, the euro zone should concentrate on making it easier to restructure unpayable debt. Banks should issue contingent convertible bonds that can turn debt into equity when they get into trouble, so absorbing losses. And sovereign bonds should include provisions for maturities to be extended when debt exceeds a certain level. By contrast, the Glienicker group, a collection of 11 pro-European German economists, lawyers and political scientists, is pushing for a stronger dose of federalism.[6] It calls for a "robust" banking union, a "controlled transfer mechanism" including common unemployment insurance and a common budget to promote public goods. Similar conclusions were reached by a French gathering calling itself the "Eiffel Group".[7] Economic logic points to greater federalism in fiscal and banking affairs. But political reality is that the wallet, and the power to tax, will remain national. The euro zone will therefore remain hybrid for the foreseeable future.

Besides the risk of political backlash against economic governance, there are other reasons to worry that the current model is unstable. The ECB's position as lender of last resort remains ambiguous. Mario Draghi's great bluff, the OMT policy, may not hold forever. Moreover, the ECB's one-size-fits-all interest rate is a one-size-fits-none arrangement that has a tendency to amplify economic divergence. It is now too low for Germany and too high for Mediterranean countries, whereas the situations were reversed when the euro began in 1999. Similar arguments apply to the common exchange rate, which has tended to favour high-end German exports over, for example, more price-sensitive Italian ones. Some worry that, as a result of the crisis money, production capacity and skilled workers are shifting permanently to core economies through the so-called "agglomeration effect", with no transfers to soften the blow to the periphery.

Without a large American-style federal budget, countries of the euro zone need other means to adjust: more flexible markets for labour, products and services; greater mobility of workers; and more cross-border ownership of assets. But in all these respects, EU countries are a lot less integrated than the United States. The principal shock absorber is national borrowing. But in times of high debt, borrowing is a limited instrument, and may even be counterproductive if markets doubt a country's solvency.

The IMF notes that federations such as the United States, Canada and Germany are able to absorb about 80% of economic shocks in their states or provinces,[8] whereas the euro zone manages to smooth just 40% of asymmetric shocks. In other words, a 1% drop in GDP results in household consumption shrinking by 0.2% in federations and 0.6% in the euro zone. It is thus apparent that the euro zone should become, in some aspects, more federal if the euro is to function more effectively. As in the United States or Canada, the aim should be to create a European system that is resilient enough to allow each country to make its own choices, and bear the consequences when things go wrong. Discipline is best exerted by markets, not Eurocrats. As the IMF paper notes, no-bail-out rules are more credible when there are risk-sharing mechanisms to contain the impact of default.

Seen this way, more federalism in some domains is a means of restoring choice to governments, not of taking it away. It would relieve deficit countries of ever more intrusive central controls, and surplus countries of the duty to rescue others. Fiscal federalism does not imply that the EU (or euro zone) has to become the United States of Europe. Some powers could and should be repatriated as part of the bargain. Forget about a European army (it would never leave barracks) or a single EU seat at the UN. Europe does not need to speak with one voice. But it needs the euro zone to operate as one coherent financial system. Precisely how far integration must go remains something of a guessing game. But here are a few priorities.

Complete banking union

Begin with a real banking union. The euro zone's trouble started as a banking crisis and, in contrast with the United States, it has yet to be resolved. The uncertainty over unseen losses in banks is hampering recovery. A new supervisor has been created and bail-in rules have been agreed. Germany has belatedly agreed to a complex bank-resolution mechanism and a pooled bank-resolution fund, paid for by banks, that will be created over several years. That is a precedent for mutualisation.

It is right that banks and their creditors bear the brunt of bank failures. But to become stable, banking union needs a taxpayer-funded backstop if a big crisis strikes. A common deposit-insurance system would help to provide greater stability. A half-baked banking union will not break the vicious circle between weak banks and weak sovereigns.

Cut unpayable debt

Sovereign debt is the other end of bank-sovereign loop. It has risen to its highest level since the second world war, and at the beginning of

2014 stood at 95% of GDP on average in the euro zone – Greece was at 176%, Italy at 133%. Private debt is also high in many countries.

One lesson of the crisis, especially in Greece, is the need for a clear-eyed distinction between problems of liquidity and problems of solvency. Fudging the assessment of a country's debt and hoping for the best is a bad choice for debtor and creditor alike. In any future bail-out it is better to cut unpayable debt from the outset. The losses would thus fall on those that lent the money to uncreditworthy countries. Adjustment programmes need to have sufficient margins to deal with problems when forecasts inevitably go wrong. It is better for a country to exceed its targets than consistently undershoot them.

Having made the error, official creditors should lift the burden on Greece, as promised, now that it has reached a primary budget surplus (that is, before interest payments). A debt write-off would be better than an endless process of "extend and pretend" that leaves a perpetual cloud of uncertainty over Greece. The sooner and more explicitly it is done, the stronger the signal to markets that Greece is coming out of its misery.

Moreover, a similar principle could be extended to other rescued countries: the terms of their bail-out loans should be softened once they have got into primary surplus. This is especially justified in the case of Ireland, which was prevented from wiping out senior bondholders of its bust banks, even though this has become an aim of banking union. Italy, Europe's biggest debtor, needs to embark on sustained privatisation to pay off debt and encourage more competition.

Other measures to make it easier to restructure debt, both private and public, would be sensible.

Bond together

In the longer term, the euro zone should move towards some form of mutualisation of debt. One reason is to limit excessive borrowing costs; another is to send a political signal of commitment to the common currency; a third is to create a safe asset for banks to hold, so helping to break the doom-loop with sovereigns.

There are now many proposals for Eurobonds. A 2010 paper by Jakob von Weizsäcker and Jacques Delpla for the Bruegel think-tank in

Brussels proposes a hybrid "blue bond, red bond" system: countries would issue joint bonds, guaranteed jointly and severally by all euro-zone members (blue bonds), up to the "good" debt threshold of 60% of GDP; beyond that countries would issue riskier national bonds (red bonds). Another idea, proposed by the German government's official council of economic advisers, was inspired by Alexander Hamilton: it would pool the "bad" debt above the Maastricht threshold in a temporary debt redemption fund that would be guaranteed by all, with a commitment by each member to pay off its share over 20 years.[9] The latter is less complicated in legal terms and may be a good starting point. If such an assumption of debt could be achieved with another Hamiltonian touch, by simultaneously restructuring the debt to lighten the burden, it would be even better.

But such ideas for common bonds run into a huge objection: why should the thrifty guarantee debts accumulated by the profligate? Texas does not stand behind California's debt. American treasuries are federal debt, paid for by federal taxes. Embryonic forms of European debt already exist, such as bonds issued by the rescue funds. But granting European institutions the authority to issue debt and raise taxes would be contentious. Euro-zone "treasuries" could start in a limited manner, for instance by issuing short-dated bills. Moral hazard is a real problem; after all, the euro zone's imbalances built up at a time when markets behaved as if Eurobonds were already in existence. Clear qualification criteria could mitigate the risk and give countries good reasons to reform. Vulnerable countries need incentives as well as threats and rules to stick to the path of reform.

The need to balance

So far the burden of adjustment has been placed mainly on deficit countries, while Germany's current-account surplus has continued to grow (see Figure 12.4), to the point where the US Treasury complains that it is hampering recovery, both in the euro zone and globally.

In an open trading area the connection between Germany's surplus and other countries' deficits is complex. Boosting demand in Germany – say by increasing investment, allowing wages to rise or granting a tax cut – might suck imports from the United States, China or eastern

FIG 12.4 **A long climb**
Current-account balance, 2004–14, % of GDP

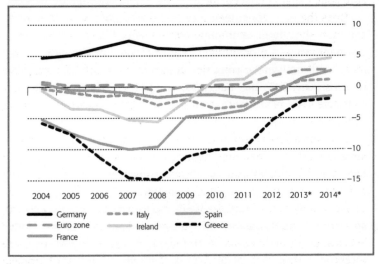

*Forecast
Sources: Eurostat; European Commission

Europe more than from the Mediterranean. Even so it would help, not least because it could help to weaken the euro's exchange rate (though a better way of achieving this would be through looser monetary policy). In political terms, though, unless Germany is seen to do more to help the euro zone's economic rebalancing, it will face stronger calls for some system of permanent fiscal transfers. It is striking that China has done more to reduce its surplus and rebalance the global economy, by raising its exchange rate and stimulating the economy, than Germany.

A stronger centre

Fully fledged federations have a central budget that provides public goods and redistributes income between rich and poor citizens (and states). The budget helps to absorb the shock when one or other region suffers a downturn. Even when local tax revenues drop, the federal government continues to spend on defence, capital projects, unemployment insurance and, often, health care. Federal budgets invariably act as the backstop for the banks. By contrast, the EU has a tiny budget, no power of taxation and no powers to borrow. And the euro zone has no budget at all.

Does the euro zone need a central pot of money? France wants common short-term unemployment benefits across the euro zone. Germany wants a more limited and conditional model: providing at most small transfers to countries as part of "contracts" for structural reforms. The IMF has suggested a modest "rainy-day" fund, a collective savings account that could make transfers when countries suffer a downturn.

But even a small fund runs into a big obstacle. Euro-zone countries already have large national budgets, consuming about 50% of GDP. Spending by federal and state governments in the United States amounts to just 38% of GDP, and 33% of GDP in Switzerland. The EU's budget amounts to about 1% of GDP. Measured another way, federal spending accounts for 55% of total public spending in the United States and 43% in Switzerland. The 1977 MacDougall report suggested a central budget of 5–7% of GDP in the early stages of a European federation. Even Canada's relatively small federal government accounts for 34% of total public spending. The equivalent figure for the EU is currently 2% of GDP. Any euro-zone fund would therefore require adding to an already heavy tax burden, or shifting spending from national to European level, or sharply cutting the rest of the EU budget. None of these would be easy.

The IMF thinks a euro-zone rainy-day fund, made up of annual contributions of between 1.5% and 2.5% of GDP (that is, about twice as large as the EU's budget), would be enough to give the euro zone a similar level of shock-absorption as other federations and would roughly even out transfers over time. Had it been created in 1999, almost all countries (except tiny Luxembourg, which boasts the EU's richest population) would have received roughly the same as they had put in. Germany would have benefited when it was regarded as the "sick man of Europe". Such an automatic system would provide more timely help than a bail-out fund and avoid disputes over conditions imposed on recipients. If the European fund could also issue bonds, it could run a counter-cyclical European-level economic policy during a general recession, making it easier for countries to stick to balanced-budget rules.

The problem with a rainy-day fund is that it is hard to assess the economic cycle in real time, so deciding when to make payments, and how large they should be, could be tricky. The French idea of an unemployment-insurance system could act as a proxy. National governments would still pay for long-term joblessness, which reflects national labour-market rigidities, while a European fund could top up benefits for the first six months of unemployment that are more likely to reflect the short-term cycle. It is unlikely that Germany would ever agree to this without a high degree of harmonisation in labour-market practices. The Glienicker group would extend unemployment insurance only to "countries that organise their labour market in line with the needs of the monetary union". Yet done properly and with clear limits and conditions, such a system could satisfy France's desire for a "social" dimension to Europe and Germany's insistence on labour-market reforms with the euro-zone's need for mobility of workers.

A more central bank

Visible progress towards integration would give the ECB greater confidence to intervene as a guardian of the euro while reforms are enacted. If a future euro-zone fund acted as a backstop for banks and issued European debt, the ECB could increasingly act as a lender of last resort to the European fund, rather than to national governments, thus freeing it from the uncomfortable business of setting conditions, directly or indirectly, in return for monetary action to help vulnerable countries.

As supervisor of euro-zone banks, the ECB should ensure that bond holdings are diversified and encourage cross-border bank mergers, to help break the doom-loop between banks and sovereigns. And given that its supervisory role already raises questions about its political independence, not least because bank failures have an impact on national treasuries, the ECB should get out of the entanglement of the troika.

For now, the ECB must have the courage to loosen monetary policy more aggressively, despite German complaints that savings are being undermined, to avert the threat of deflation. A dose of American-style quantitative easing may be in order. Once again, though, it would be easier if the ECB had Eurobonds to buy instead of having to pick and choose which country's debt to buy and which to exclude.

Narrow the democratic deficit

The integration of the euro zone, the intrusion of European bodies into national economic policymaking and the growing popular disenchantment with the European project require the democratic deficit to be addressed more urgently than ever.

But for the foreseeable future – for as long as real power, budgetary authority and legitimacy lie with national governments – it is best to enhance the role of national parliaments and perhaps even downgrade that of the European Parliament. This can be done by giving national parliaments greater authority to scrutinise the decisions taken by national ministers, prime ministers and presidents in Brussels. National parliaments can also be given greater powers to veto or modify European legislation. Moreover, there could be scope for a joint body of national MPs to examine inter-governmental decisions, such as bail-out decisions by the troika and the Eurogroup.

Giving the system greater national democratic legitimacy would be a huge step in the right direction. But even this may not be enough to legitimise the full panoply of measures and procedures in the European semester and its associated pacts. If, as seems likely, national politics at some stage reasserts itself by reclaiming fiscal and economic autonomy from Brussels, it will be that much more important for parliaments to understand the European repercussions of national economic policies. Germany realised this when it insisted that debt brakes be introduced in national legislation through the fiscal compact.

If the euro zone were ever to adopt truly federal elements, for instance if it were given a central budget or the power to raise taxes, these powers would certainly need to be held to account by the European Parliament. At that point there may even be scope for the direct election of some jobs in Brussels. For now, the indirect election of candidates for president of the European Commission, as envisaged by the European Parliament, is a travesty. Voters are not being offered a real chance to influence EU policies, but the experiment with

Spitzenkandidaten (leading candidates) risks calling into question the impartiality of the Commission on a whole series of functions where it needs to act as a referee – not least in assessing the economic policies of individual countries.

A fitter Commission

The Commission remains the engine of the EU. But enlargement of the union has turned the cosy old college system into an unwieldy bureaucracy with 28 commissioners, each a little baron seeking to push pet projects, resulting in legislative overreach. Especially as the Commission gains powers to influence national economic policies, it should get out of the business of setting out the minutiae of regulation. The so-called REFIT initiative to cut red tape, such as a silly proposal to ban hairdressers from wearing high heels, is a good start. But much more can be done to make a reality of José Manuel Barroso's dictum that "the EU needs to be big on big things, and smaller on smaller things". That said, deepening the single market by necessity requires European-level regulation, if only to cut through the thickets of 28 different sets of national laws.

It is time to revive the notion of a more streamlined Commission, perhaps by having senior and junior commissioners, which might make it easier to slim down the volume of Commission activity – so long as it can free itself from the control of the European Parliament, which favours more legislation, not less. The Germans and the British have also suggested that all draft legislation, whether directives or regulations, should be dropped at the end of every term of a Commission, as happens in most national legislatures.[10]

If governments want a good Commission, a good place to start would be for them to appoint competent commissioners rather than use Brussels as a dumping ground for second-division political hacks.

Chart the course

Creating a more stable and integrated euro zone will require several big bargains – between creditors and debtors, between older and newer members, between euro ins and outs. There will need to be much more Europe in some areas in return for much less in others.

And as the euro zone integrates, there should be more integration of the single market. To navigate through these treacherous waters, European countries need a clearer destination. The Monnet method of integration step-by-step, sector-by-sector, with an ambiguous final objective, is reaching its limits. The euro now affects the core of national politics, so it cannot be delegated to technocrats indefinitely. The system will need more democracy and accountability, though how this is achieved may ultimately differ between the euro zone and the wider EU. Herman Van Rompuy, president of the European Council, was thinking along the right lines when he appointed himself to draw up his abortive road map for a "genuine economic and monetary union".

Members of the euro zone do not yet trust each other enough to take on big liabilities in one leap. Reform will have to be done in stages to build confidence. To borrow Schäuble's phrase about banking union, there could first be a "wooden" structure, followed by a steel one. But if debtors are to agree to more discipline, they need confidence that a system of greater solidarity will follow.

Germany has every reason to worry about moral hazard. Weak countries might fail to reform once market pressure is lifted. But moral hazard applies to the strong too: no sooner had fear of the euro's break-up subsided than Germany started to water down banking union. A plan for greater sharing of liabilities matched by the restoration of a credible no-bail-out rule could prove an attractive bargain.

One problem is that many changes would require treaty change. Most leaders, like the institutions in Brussels, recoil at the idea of a big negotiation and multiple referendums at a time when voters are restive, populists are on the rise and incumbents in trouble almost everywhere. Germany, conscious of the strictures of its constitutional court, is more open to reform through a succession of small revisions under the "simplified procedure" that requires fewer referendums. But such piecemeal reforms may not provide scope for the necessary compromises. And there is always reluctance to give the UK the opportunity to complicate things with demands for repatriation of powers.

A full treaty negotiation may be inevitable, even desirable, in

2015 and 2016 to settle some fundamental questions and to explore whether the minimum that the UK can accept can be reconciled with the maximum that other EU countries are prepared to offer. But if the process gets bogged down, one way around these difficulties is to negotiate inter-governmental deals outside the EU's treaties. EU purists and the European Parliament intensely dislike inter-governmentalism. It detracts from the "community method", it denies power to the Parliament and it creates more opportunity for big countries to bully smaller ones. But the accords establishing the European Stability Mechanism (ESM) in 2011 and the fiscal compact in 2012, both inter-governmental treaties, were negotiated easily and quickly. And they brought an important innovation, common in other international treaties (and indeed in the constitution of the United States), of coming into force once a threshold number of ratifications was reached, that is, without the requirement for unanimity. This reduces the scope for angry holdouts, be they referendum voters or obstreperous parliaments, to block everything. The ESM is already a common fund that can borrow on markets, so could easily be expanded to incorporate other functions.

Greater integration in the euro zone is bound to increase tensions between the 18 ins and the ten outs. But relations would be worse still if the euro zone failed to right itself. The task will be to bind the euro zone closer together within the wider EU. The trick is that integration of the euro zone should go hand-in-hand with deepening the single market. But beyond this, safeguards will be needed to ensure that the ins do not gang up on the outs, and that the euro zone's policies are open to newcomers. It is hard to see the euro zone consistently voting as a block, but the habit of co-ordination, and the fact that most countries still want to join the euro, will worry the remaining outs.

The UK's future status is an acute headache that could come to dominate much European business. Unlike most outs, the UK is half out of the EU as a whole, and David Cameron is proposing a referendum on its EU membership in 2017. The UK has dithered over his demands in a renegotiation, partly because it does not know what might be on offer. But a more complete single market, ambitious trade deals, lighter EU regulation, curbing benefits for migrants and a smaller EU budget (say if farm spending were cut to make room for a euro-zone fund) might be achievable. The departure of the UK would be a grave loss, not just for the UK but also for the EU. Euro-zone countries need to liberalise markets, both to promote growth and to enhance their ability to adjust wages and prices. The UK's liberalising zeal would be invaluable.

The twin dangers ahead

Which way is Europe heading? Its leaders have shown they will act to avoid imminent shipwreck. This means that a sudden, catastrophic default and currency redenomination is improbable. For the same reason, countries are unlikely to heed Trichet's exhortations, at the start of the crisis, to "immediately jump into political union". Even the more focused reforms proposed above are unlikely to happen spontaneously. Many will see the economic sense in such changes, but they come with a political cost to some or all governments. This means that leaders will act only when compelled to do so by events. The most likely course is to drift, with periods of crisis and piecemeal reforms, followed by more drift.

The next crisis – and there will surely be a next crisis – could come from any number of directions. It could be triggered, as at the outset, by a problem in the banks. The euro zone's financial sector has had much capital injected into it but banks remain wobbly. A succession of discredited stress tests means that nobody quite knows how many more losses are lurking in bank balance sheets. The ECB's review of banks' assets, due to be completed in 2014, might discover losses that sovereigns are unable to bear and the euro zone is unwilling to take on.

The forthcoming turmoil might be precipitated by doubts cast on the one policy that has most decisively halted any looming collapse: the ECB's promise to intervene in bond markets if needed to stop the euro from breaking up. The policy of OMT could yet be undermined by the latest (or a future) adverse ruling in Germany's constitutional court. Enacting OMT requires countries to seek, and receive, a rescue programme from the ESM, and often parliamentary votes. Would the Bundestag vote knowing it might unleash the ECB against the will of the Bundesbank and the Karlsruhe court? Would the Bundesbank comply with ECB demands to buy bonds? Conversely, will the ECB stand back if the euro is in danger and politicians fail to act? Nobody knows whether the ECB, in setting no limit for bond purchases, is genuinely ready to buy unlimited amounts of debt. In truth, the ECB's policy of OMT is a bit like a nuclear weapon: a deterrent that may work best if it is never tested.

The two most obvious dangers to the euro zone are economic and political. The euro zone faces a long period of stagnation. Weak recovery means that countries will struggle to reduce mass joblessness in parts of southern Europe, and they could more easily be pushed into a triple-dip recession. If that happens, what chance is there that their people will put up with another round of austerity and Brussels-imposed "economic governance"? Japanese-style deflation was a growing worry in 2014. In short, the market's optimism in early 2014 about the prospects for peripheral economies seemed overdone; bad news could bring a sudden reassessment, just as it did in 2010.

Even without such grim scenarios, slow growth and high unemployment are already radicalising politics and intensifying rejection of both national and European politicians. So the next crisis may well be political. Anti-EU, anti-immigrant and anti-establishment parties of all colours are on the rise. The European elections – usually a sideshow – of May 2014 are an important moment. The rise of populist parties may point to a pressing need to reform the system; yet their strength might also make sensible changes hard or even impossible. Anti-EU parties are divided among themselves, and often more interested in megaphone (or YouTube) politics than in the detail of policy. Their direct impact on legislation in Brussels may therefore be limited, beyond making the European Parliament noisier. But the populist parties could change national political dynamics in several countries, so affecting European policies more indirectly. Governments may feel under pressure to halt reforms, be they national or at the European level.

Thereafter, a national election in the south, say in Greece, could return a constellation of parties that refuses to comply with bail-out conditions or decides that leaving the euro is the lesser evil. Or an exasperated creditor country in the north, say the Netherlands, might refuse to pay for the next bail-out or just reject the debt restructuring that Greece needs. Or the trouble might come from a non-euro country, for instance if a British referendum were to come down in favour of leaving the EU, disrupting the whole system. Or important countries might just fail to muster the political support for long-delayed economic reforms. Italy is the perennial backmarker in economic growth. For many governments, Jean-Claude Juncker's dictum about structural reforms still holds: "We all know what to do, we just don't know how to get re-elected after we've done it." Even at the height of the crisis, and led by the reform-minded Mario Monti, the Italian government found it easier to raise taxes and cut spending than challenge vested interests by enacting structural reforms. In France, François Hollande has belatedly promised some still-vague supply-side reforms, but he may be too enfeebled to deliver. With the far-right National Front gaining ground, France remains a cause of acute anxiety in both Germany and Brussels.

All these risks offer good reasons for early action on the reforms set out here. A sense of direction towards integration, even if slow and conditional, would help stabilise the euro zone, restore confidence in markets that it is being repaired, provide incentives for reform and give citizens in the most stricken countries a sense of hope for a better future. It could help avoid the next crisis, or at least mitigate its impact. But Europe's leaders have not proven to be endowed with long-term vision. So the best that can probably be hoped for is that the euro zone lurches from one crisis-induced reform to another. This will be unnecessarily costly and painful, but might somehow lead to a more coherent and workable system. But there is another possibility: that the euro zone, and the EU with it, will stumble from one crisis to the next until, exhausted, one or all of its members lose the will to preserve the single currency, and perhaps the wider project.

Europeans like to point out that it took the United States more than two centuries, many crises and a civil war before it fully developed its model of federalism. To judge from the repeated flirtation with self-inflicted default, the US system could still be perfected. Europe can therefore be forgiven if it moves slowly and uncertainly. For all its flaws, the EU can claim to have helped support peace among its members for more than six decades.

Europe's model, if it survives, will be different from that of the United States. Europe is an older continent, with a more heterogeneous population and a deeper sense of distinct national histories. As well as the push for European integration, there is a counter-current of disaggregation. Well before the UK holds its referendum on EU membership, Scotland will hold a ballot in September 2014 on whether to remain within the UK. Catalonia is demanding a similar right to hold a referendum on whether to remain part of Spain.

So there will not be a United States of Europe, and nor need there be. That said, Europeans should not waste the opportunity to learn from others what works and what does not, particularly when it comes to currency unions.

A question of (German) history

Europe's course will depend, in large part, on Germany – Europe's most powerful economy and biggest creditor. In many ways, the question of the euro comes back to the old question of Germany, a country too strong to live with easily yet not strong enough to dominate permanently (or, indeed, to rescue everybody). The single currency, like the European Union, was meant to reconcile Germany with its old enemies and harness its strength for the benefit of the continent.

Germany needs a political strategy for Europe. It has been conditioned to avoid any notion of leadership. But lead it must. Failure to do so also has consequences. Angela Merkel has won a third term and the respect of many Europeans. She is a pragmatic politician, not a visionary one. Her favourite dictum is "step-by-step". It is time for her to say where she wants to go.

In 2014 the world looks back 100 years to commemorate the cataclysm of the first of two world wars, in which the heart of the matter was the power of Germany. Two works of history conclude by reflecting on the lessons for today's leaders. In one, published in 2012, Christopher Clark notes:[11]

> The actors in the euro-zone crisis, like those in 1914, were aware that there was a possible outcome that would be generally catastrophic (the failure of the euro). All the key protagonists hoped this would not happen, but in addition to this shared interest, they all had special – and conflicting – interests of their own.

In the second, published in 2013, Brendan Simms asks, more pointedly:[12]

> Will Berlin come to accept that the alternative to a democratically controlled European currency is a German economic hegemony that will in the long run destroy the European Union? ... If that happens, history will judge the European Union an expensive youthful prank which the continent played in its dotage.

The fathers of the European Union felt the weight of history. This was still true of the Kohl-Mitterrand generation that created the euro. But today's crop of leaders, for the most part, sees the problems, inconvenience, constraints and threat of Europe, rather than its promise. Perhaps they lack the memory of war, and have lost the fear of history's judgment. Or perhaps now that war seems inconceivable an older history can reassert itself, one in which old nations do not easily abandon their powers, prerogatives and sense of identity. Or perhaps the European project has been so long in the making that it has lost its romance.

There is an asymmetry about Europe's crisis. The euro has the potential to destroy the European project. Yet saving the single currency is a poor rallying-cry for European integration. So pressure from markets brings only short-term expedients, not a design for the future. Europe's leaders fear undoing European integration, but dare not promote it either.

Something of great value may thus be lost through carelessness or timidity. The best way to gauge the achievements of the European Union is to visit its eastern borderlands. The EU has helped to solidify post-communist democracies, many of which are among the fastest-growing economies in Europe. Here countries are still lining up to join the euro, flawed as it may be, because of the economic and political security it still offers in an uncertain region. Just beyond, countries are knocking at the door to be admitted to the EU. The countries of the western Balkans, many of them traumatised by the violent break-up of the former Yugoslavia, are still lured by the idea of belonging to Europe's community of democracies. In Ukraine, protesters have for months held up the EU's blue flag as a symbol of freedom. Despite scores of people being shot dead in Kiev, they toppled a corrupt and inept government – and provoked a Russian military intervention whose outcome remains uncertain – in the attempt to draw their country closer to Europe.

Europe's malaise is not one that time alone can heal. Delay is likely to make things worse, not better. Though the financial panic is in abeyance, the economic and political crises are far from over, and may well deepen. Right now the political momentum is towards fragmentation, not integration. Unless the euro zone is redesigned with greater determination, in particular through greater risk-sharing, it is unlikely to recover economic vitality. And unless the euro can be shown to deliver prosperity and well-being, public support for the European Union will inexorably ebb away.

Notes

Preface

1   Leonard, M., *Why Europe will run the 21st Century*, Public Affairs (2005)

1 If the euro fails, Europe fails

1   Meyer, T., *Der Geuro: Eine Parallelwährung für Griechenland?* (in German), Deutsche Bank, May 2012, available at: www.dbresearch.de/PROD/ DBR_INTERNET_DE-PROD/PROD0000000000288868.pdf. Some of Meyer's arguments are reported in *Business Insider*, available at: www. businessinsider.com/introducing-the-geuro-a-new-parallel-currency-to-solve-all-of-greeces-problems-2012-5. Meyer himself sets out some of his views in this piece for the *Wall Street Journal*, available at: online.wsj. com/news/articles/SB10001424127887324556304578116830518460210

2   Roger Bootle *et al.*, *Leaving the Euro: A Practical Guide*, Capital Economics, revised submission to the 2012 Wolfson Prize. This and other submissions are available at: www.policyexchange.org.uk/images/ WolfsonPrize/wolfson%20economics%20prize%20winning%20entry.pdf

3   See "Tempted, Angela?" at www.economist.com/node/21560269

4   See page 22 of Gill, I.S. and Raiser, M., *Golden Growth: Restoring the Lustre of the European economic model*, World Bank, 2012 (overview) http:// www-wds.worldbank.org/external/default/WDSContentServer/WDSP/ IB/2013/11/15/000442464_20131115123906/Rendered/PDF/681680PUB0v10 G00Box379791B00PUBLIC0.pdf

2 From the origins to Maastricht

1   Churchill Zurich speech available at: www.churchill-society-london.org. uk/astonish.html

2   Schuman speech available at: europa.eu/about-eu/basic-information/ symbols/europe-day/schuman-declaration/

3   European Coal and Steel Community available at: europa.eu/ legislation_summaries/institutional_affairs/treaties/treaties_ecsc_en.htm

4   Quoted by Otmar Issing, July 2nd 2013, available
    at: www.project-syndicate.org/commentary/
    the-risk-of-european-centralization-by-otmar-issing
5   See Dell, E., *The Schuman Plan and the British Abdication of Leadership in
    Europe*, Oxford University Press, 1995, p. 169.
6   Quoted in *In with the Euro, Out with the Pound* by Christopher Johnson
    (Penguin Books, 1996).
7   Crafts, N., *Saving the Euro: a Pyrrhic Victory*, available at: www.
    chathamhouse.org/publications/papers/view/195771
8   This story is told in *The Official History of Britain and the European
    Community, Volume II* by Stephen Wall (Routledge, 2013).
9   This section has drawn on *Making the European Monetary Union* by
    Harold James (Harvard University Press, 2012) and *The Euro: the Battle for
    the New Global Currency* by David Marsh (Yale University Press, 2011).
10 Mundell, R., *A Theory of Optimum Currency Areas*, available at: www.
    aeaweb.org/aer/top20/51.4.657-665.pdf
11 Report of a study group on the role of public finance in European
    integration, available at: ec.europa.eu/economy_finance/emu_history/
    documentation/chapter8/19770401en73macdougallrepvol1.pdf
12 The story of the single market and the path to 1992 is told in *Europe
    Relaunched: Truths and Illusions on the Way to 1992* by Nicolas Colchester
    and David Buchan (Hutchison, 1990).
13 David Cameron, speech to World Economic Forum in
    Davos, January 26th 2012, available at: www.politics.co.uk/
    comment-analysis/2012/01/26/david-cameron-s-davos-speech-in-full
14 "Banking on a crisis?", *The Economist*, October 29th 1998, available at:
    www.economist.com/node/174327
15 Reported in www.causeur.fr/%C2%AB-on-ne-rejette-pas-platon-
    %C2%BB,12999

3 How it all works

1   Appendix 2 summarises the main treaties, regulations and pacts
    governing the European Union and the euro.
2   This section has drawn on the two best general guides to the European
    Union: *The Penguin Companion to European Union* by Anthony Teasdale
    and Timothy Bainbridge (4th edition, Penguin, 2012) and *Guide to the
    European Union* by Dick Leonard (10th edition, Profile Books, 2010 –
    11th edition due in 2014). See also *The Passage to Europe* by Luuk van
    Middelaar (Yale University Press, 2013), especially for the early years of
    the European project.

3   The argument was set out in "The Stability Pact: More than a Minor
     Nuisance" by Barry Eichengreen and Charles Wyplosz in Begg, D. *et al.*
     (eds), *EMU: Prospects and Challenges for the Euro*, Blackwell, 1998.
4   See "Farewell to the stupidity pact", October 22nd 2002, available at:
     www.economist.com/node/1402102
5   The story of the constitutional treaty is told in two books: *The Accidental
     Constitution* by Peter Norman (Eurocomment, 2005) and *The Struggle for
     Europe's Constitution* by Andrew Duff (Federal Trust, 2005).
6   On the British budget question, see among others, *A Stranger in Europe*
     by Stephen Wall (Oxford University Press, 2008) and *Britain's Quest for a
     Role* by David Hannay (I.B. Tauris, 2013).

4 Build-up to a crisis

1   Gill, I.S. and Raiser, M., *Golden Growth: Restoring the Lustre of the
     European economic model*, World Bank, 2012, see www.worldbank.org/
     en/region/eca/publication/golden-growth
2   Gros, D., *Will EMU survive 2010?*, Centre for European Policy Studies,
     2006, available at: www.ceps.be/ceps/dld/3059/pdf
3   Tilford, S., *Will the Eurozone Crack?*, Centre for European Reform,
     September 2006, available at: www.cer.org.uk/sites/default/files/
     publications/attachments/pdf/2011/p_688_eurozone_crack_42-892.pdf
4   Véron, N., *Is Europe Ready for a Major Banking Crisis?*, Bruegel,
     August 2007, available at: www.bruegel.org/download/
     parent/234-is-europe-ready-for-a-major-banking-crisis/
     file/659-is-europe-ready-for-a-major-banking-crisis-english/
5   *EMU@10: Successes and challenges after ten years of Economic and
     Monetary Union*, European Commission, available at: ec.europa.eu/
     economy_finance/publications/publication12682_en.pdf
6   Delors, J., *Report on economic and monetary union in the European
     Community*, April 1989, available at: ec.europa.eu/economy_finance/
     publications/publication6161_en.pdf

5 Trichet's test

1   Article 125: "A Member State shall not be liable for or assume the
     commitments of central governments, regional, local or other public
     authorities, other bodies governed by public law, or public undertakings
     of another Member State, without prejudice to mutual financial
     guarantees for the joint execution of a specific project."
2   Article 122.2: "Where a Member State is in difficulties or is seriously
     threatened with severe difficulties caused by natural disasters or
     exceptional occurrences beyond its control, the Council, on a proposal
     from the Commission, may grant, under certain conditions, Union

financial assistance to the Member State concerned. The President of the Council shall inform the European Parliament of the decision taken."

3   The details were reported by the *Wall Street Journal* more than three years after the event, based on a leak of the board minutes, see: online. wsj.com/news/articles/SB10001424052702304441404579119180237594344. The excerpts from the minutes are worth reading at: blogs.wsj.com/economics/2013/10/07/imf-document-excerpts-disagreements-revealed/

4   An account of the ECB's actions in this key weekend of May 2010 is given in *The Alchemists: Three Central Bankers and the World on Fire* by Neil Urwin, Viking Press, 2013. An extract was printed by the *Washington Post* at: www.washingtonpost.com/business/three-days-that-saved-the-world-financial-system/2013/03/28/d5b9a38c-94ef-11e2-b6f0-a5150a247b6a_print.html

5   "E-Bonds would end the crisis", op-ed in the *Financial Times*, available at: www.ft.com/cms/s/0/540d41c2-009f-11e0-aa29-00144feab49a. html#axzz2mdxfF3bW

6 Super Mario

1   "Standard & Poor's Takes Various Rating Actions On 16 Eurozone Sovereign Governments" January 13th 2012, available at: www.standardandpoors.com/ratings/articles/en/us/?assetID=1245327295020

2   *Towards a Genuine Economic and Monetary Union*, available at: ec.europa.eu/economy_finance/crisis/documents/131201_en.pdf

3   Euro Area Summit Statement, June 29th 2012, available at: www.consilium.europa.eu/uedocs/cms_data/docs/pressdata/en/ec/131359.pdf

4   Berlusconi denies describing the chancellor as *una culona inchiavabile* (an "unfuckable fat-arse"), though his supporters are happy to allude to the term. See *Il Fatto Quotidiano* at: www.ilfattoquotidiano.it/2011/09/10/cucu-la-merkel-e-%E2%80%9Cinchiavabile%E2%80%9D/156545/

5   Moody's announcement on July 23rd 2012, available at: www.moodys.com/research/Moodys-changes-the-outlook-to-negative-on-Germany-Netherlands-Luxembourg--PR_251214

6   Speech by Mario Draghi, president of the European Central Bank, at the Global Investment Conference in London, July 26th 2012, available at: www.ecb.europa.eu/press/key/date/2012/html/sp120726.en.html

7   "Money Creation and Responsibility", speech by Jens Weidmann, September 18th 2012, available at: www.bundesbank.de/Redaktion/EN/Reden/2012/2012_09_20_weidmann_money_creaktion_and_responsibility.html

8   "Banking union must be built on firm foundations", Wolfgang Schäuble, *Financial Times*, May 12th 2013, available at: www.ft.com/cms/s/0/8bdaf6e8-b89f-11e2-869f-00144feabdc0.html#axzz2uvQwaeg2

7 The changing balance of power

1 The best account of the Delors period is *Delors: Inside the House that Jacques Built* by Charles Grant (Nicholas Brealey, 1994).

2 One of the first proponents of getting parliamentary groups to nominate their candidates for the presidency of the Commission was Simon Hix in *What's Wrong with Europe and How to Fix It* (Polity, 2008)

3 See article on extremist parties in Europe published in *The Economist*, January 4th 2014, available at: www.economist.com/news/briefing/21592666-parties-nationalist-right-are-changing-terms-european-political-debate-does

4 This is discussed in *Can Germany be Saved?* by Hans-Werner Sinn, available at: www.cesifo-group.de/ifoHome/publications/individual-publications/Germany/Can-Germany-Be-Saved.html

5 See "Europe's new pecking order", available at: www.economist.com/node/13610767

6 A point made in "France: a Country in Denial", available at: www.economist.com/node/21551478

7 Heisbourg, F., *La Fin du Rêve Européen*, Stock, 2013.

8 Reported at: www.spiegel.de/international/europe/now-europe-is-speaking-german-merkel-ally-demands-that-britain-contribute-to-eu-success-a-798009.html

9 A comment on this speech is available at: www.zukunftsdebatte.eu/home/aktuell/news//ecfr-why-poland-is-the-new-france-for-germany/

8 In, out, shake it all about

1 Tindemans, L., *A Report on European Union*, available at: bookshop.europa.eu/en/european-union-pbCBNF76001/

2 The Schäuble-Lamers paper is available (in German) at: www.cducsu.de/upload/schaeublelamers94.pdf

3 A more recent advocate of a two-speed Europe, basing some of his arguments on the euro, is a former Council legal adviser, Jean-Claude Piris, in his book *The Future of Europe* (Cambridge University Press, 2012).

4 See "Can Angela Merkel hold Europe together", March 10th 2011, available at: www.economist.com/node/18332786/

5 Quoted at: www.economist.com/node/3194456/

6 David Cameron's speech at Bloomberg is available at: www.gov.uk/government/speeches/eu-speech-at-bloomberg

7 George Osborne's speech to Open Europe/Fresh Start conference, January 15th 2014, available at: www.gov.uk/government/speeches/extracts-from-the-chancellors-speech-on-europe

9 Democracy and its discontents

1   This section draws on the analysis in two books with identical titles: *Democracy in Europe*. One is by Larry Siedentop (Allen Lane, 2000), the other by Vivien Schmidt (Oxford University Press, 2006).
2   See Pew Global Attitudes Survey, May 2013, available at: www.pewglobal.org/2013/05/13/the-new-sick-man-of-europe-the-european-union/; and Eurobarometer, at: ec.europa.eu/public_opinion/archives/eb/eb79/eb79_publ_fr.pdf
3   Guérot, U. and Klau, T., *After Merkozy: how France and Germany can make Europe Work*, available at: ecfr.eu/page/-/ECFR56_FRANCE_GERMANY_BRIEF_AW.pdf
4   See, for example: www.globalpost.com/dispatch/news/regions/europe/130625/european-union-eastern-central-europe-accession
5   Reports on this include: www.telegraph.co.uk/finance/financialcrisis/10088005/Francois-Hollande-tells-European-Commission-it-cant-dictate-to-France.html
6   See reports on Gerrit Zalm, for example at: www.europeanvoice.com/article/imported/colourful-money-man/50233.aspx
7   German constitutional court decision, June 30th 2009, available at: www.bverfg.de/entscheidungen/es20090630_2bve000208.html
8   See CER paper by Heather Grabbe and Stefan Lehne, available at: www.cer.org.uk/publications/archive/essay/2013/2014-european-elections-why-partisan-commission-president-would-be-b; and also a note by Charles Grant, available at: www.cer.org.uk/in-the-press/how-reduce-eus-democratic-deficit
9   In his inaugural lecture at the London School of Economics, Robert Cooper advocated electing the European Commission. See: www.lse.ac.uk/newsAndMedia/videoAndAudio/channels/publicLecturesAndEvents/player.aspx?id=1585

10 How the euro spoilt any other business

1   The Commission proposals can be found at: ec.europa.eu/energy/doc/2030/com_2014_15_en.pdf
2   The eventual text of the Bolkestein directive is available at: eur-lex.europa.eu/LexUriServ/LexUriServ.do?uri=CELEX:32006L0123:EN:HTML
3   The Monti report can be found at: ec.europa.eu/bepa/pdf/monti_report_final_10_05_2010_en.pdf
4   Quoted in the Charlemagne column, October 20th 2012, see: www.economist.com/news/europe/21564851-euro-was-meant-underpin-single-market-it-may-end-up-undermining-it
5   See Pascouau, Y., *The Future of the Area of Freedom, Security And Justice*, European Policy Centre, Brussels, January 2014, available at: www.epc.eu/pub_details.php?cat_id=1&pub_id=4092

11 Europe's place in the world

1   See www.nytimes.com/1991/06/29/world/conflict-in-yugoslavia-europeans-send-high-level-team.html

2   This point is also made in *The Uncertain Legacy of Crisis: European Foreign Policy Faces the Future* by Richard Youngs (Carnegie Endowment for International Peace, 2014).

3   See "Defenceless?", Charlemagne column, December 21st 2013, available at: www.economist.com/news/europe/21591880-austerity-hollowing-out-europes-armies-defenceless

4   This led to an especially acerbic speech by the American defence secretary, Robert Gates, available at: www.defense.gov/speeches/speech.aspx?speechid=1581

5   For one example of measures on Bulgarian and Romanian immigration, see: www.ukba.homeoffice.gov.uk/eucitizens/bulgaria-romania/

6   The latest European Commission report on enlargement to Turkey is available at: ec.europa.eu/enlargement/pdf/key_documents/2013/package/tr_rapport_2013.pdf

7   Information on the European Union's eastern neighbourhood policy can be found at: www.eeas.europa.eu/enp/index_en.htm

12 After the storm

1   Schäuble, W., "Ignore the Doomsayers. Europe is being fixed", *Financial Times*, September 16th 2013, available at: www.ft.com/cms/s/0/e88c842a-1c67-11e3-a8a3-00144feab7de.html#axzz2nqL7SnRz

2   *Greece: Ex Post Evaluation of Exceptional Access under the 2010 Stand-By Arrangement*, IMF, June 2013, available at: www.imf.org/external/pubs/ft/scr/2013/cr13156.pdf

3   *Fiscal Federalism: US History for Architects of Europe's Fiscal Union*", by C. Randall Henning and Martin Kessler, Bruegel, January 2012, available at: www.bruegel.org/publications/publication-detail/publication/669-fiscal-federalism-us-history-for-architects-of-europes-fiscal-union/

4   A good summary of the federal and "mutual assurance" models is provided by Jean Pisani-Ferry in a paper (in French) for Bruegel, *Assurance Mutuelle ou Fédéralisme? la Zone Euro entre Deux Modèles*, available at: www.bruegel.org/download/parent/757-assurance-mutuelle-ou-federalisme-la-zone-euro-entre-deux-modeles/file/1623-assurance-mutuelle-ou-federalisme-la-zone-euro-entre-deux-modeles/. Some of his views are set out in English in shorter form in an op-ed for Project Syndicate, available at: www.project-syndicate.org/commentary/federalism-or-bust-for-europe-by-jean-pisani-ferry

5   Mody, A., *A Schuman Compact for the Euro Area*, Bruegel, November 29th 2013, available at: www.bruegel.org/publications/publication-detail/publication/802-a-schuman-compact-for-the-euro-area/

6   Glienicker Group, "Towards a Euro Union", op-ed in *Die Zeit*, October
     17th 2013, available in English via Bruegel at: www.bruegel.org/nc/blog/
     detail/article/1173-towards-a-euro-union/

7   *Pour une Communauté politique de l'euro*, Groupe Eiffel Europe, February
     2014. English version available at: www.bruegel.org/nc/blog/detail/
     article/1250-for-a-euro-community/

8   Allart, C. *et al.*, *Towards a Fiscal Union for the Euro Area*, IMF, September
     25th 2013. Paper and technical notes available at: www.imf.org/external/
     pubs/cat/longres.aspx?sk=40784

9   The European Commission looked at various options for "stability
     bonds" in November 2011 (ec.europa.eu/commission_2010-2014/
     president/news/documents/pdf/green_en.pdf). In the "Blue Bond"
     proposal for Bruegel, Jakob von Weizsäcker and Jacques Delpla proposed
     mutualising all "good" debt up to the Maastricht threshold of 60% of
     GDP (www.bruegel.org/publications/publication-detail/publication/403-
     the-blue-bond-proposal/). The German Council of Economic Experts
     proposed instead pooling "bad" debt above this level in a fund to
     be paid off over 20 years (www.sachverstaendigenrat-wirtschaft.de/
     aktuellesjahrsgutachten0.html).

10   Both these ideas are proposed in *How to Build a Modern European Union*
     by Charles Grant and others (Centre for European Reform, 2013).

11   Clark, C., *The Sleepwalkers: How Europe Went to War in 1914*, Allen
     Lane, 2012.

12   Simms, B., *The Struggle for Supremacy: Europe from 1453 to the Present*,
     Allen Lane, 2013.

Appendices

Appendix 1
Timeline

February 1992	Maastricht treaty signed
June 1992	Denmark says no
September 1992	ERM crisis, UK pound and Italian lira out
May 1993	Danes say yes with opt-outs
October 1993	Maastricht treaty ratified
June 1997	Stability and Growth Pact signed
January 1999	EMU begins with 11 countries
January 2001	Greece joins EMU
January 2002	Euro notes and coins introduced
November 2003	Germany and France breach stability pact. Jean-Claude Trichet becomes ECB president
August 2007	ECB liquidity injection begins
September 2008	Lehman Brothers collapses
January 2009	Greece downgraded
November 2009	New Greek government admits to bigger budget deficit
May 2010	First Greek bail-out
October 2010	Deauville deal on private-sector involvement
November 2010	Irish bail-out
May 2011	Portuguese bail-out
July 2011	Second Greek bail-out
August 2011	ECB buys Italian and Spanish bonds
October 2011	Haircut on Greek debt
November 2011	George Papandreou and Silvio Berlusconi forced out of office in Greece and Italy respectively. Mario Draghi becomes ECB president

December 2011	Draghi launches LTRO. Fiscal compact treaty agreed. Mariano Rajoy becomes Spain's prime minister
February 2012	Rajoy admits higher Spanish budget deficit
May 2012	François Hollande elected French president
June 2012	Partial bail-out agreed for Spanish banks. Agreement on banking union
July 2012	Draghi gives "whatever it takes" speech
August 2012	ECB agrees OMT programme
October 2012	Angela Merkel visits Athens
November 2012	Greek debt burden spread out, interest-rate cut
December 2012	European Council rejects Manuel Barroso and Herman Van Rompuy's plans for greater union
February 2013	Indecisive Italian election
March 2013	First Cyprus bail-out, banks shut, revised bail-out
April 2013	Enrico Letta becomes Italian prime minister
September 2013	German election. Merkel wins and negotiates grand coalition
December 2013	Ireland exits bail-out programme. Single bank supervisor agreed
January 2014	Latvia joins euro
February 2014	Matteo Renzi becomes Italian prime minister

Appendix 2
Treaties, regulations and pacts

Treaty of Rome

The founding basis for the European Economic Community (EEC) and its associated bodies. Signed in Rome by the original six countries – France, West Germany, Italy, Belgium, the Netherlands and Luxembourg – in March 1957.

Single European Act

The legal document that underpins the 1992 single market by providing for more widespread use of qualified-majority voting. Agreed in Luxembourg in December 1985, signed in February 1986 and entered into force in July 1987.

Maastricht treaty

Formally the Treaty on European Union. The founding legal document for European economic and monetary union (EMU), agreed in Maastricht in December 1991, signed in February 1992 and ratified in October 1993. The treaty lays down five "convergence criteria" to be fulfilled by candidates to join EMU. Denmark and the UK were granted opt-outs from stage three, the adoption of a single currency.

Treaty of Amsterdam

Provides the legal basis for justice and home affairs and for a common foreign and security policy to become part of the EU. Agreed in Amsterdam in June 1997 and entered into force in May 1999.

Treaty of Nice

Changed the voting weights and several EU institutions in preparation for the 2004 enlargement to take in ten new members, mainly from central and eastern Europe. Agreed in Nice in December 2000 and entered into force in February 2003.

Treaty of Lisbon

After the European constitutional treaty was rejected by referendums in 2005 in France and the Netherlands, its essential elements were subsumed into the Lisbon treaty, which was signed in December 2007 and entered into force in December 2009. The treaty changes the voting system, establishes a permanent president of the European Council and sets up a new external action service under a high representative for foreign policy.

Stability and Growth Pact

A set of regulations agreed in 1997 to impose budget discipline on euro-zone countries, with the possibility of swingeing fines on those with budget deficits over 3% of GDP. After France and Germany broke the pact in 2003–04, it was subsumed into a new excessive deficits procedure known as the six-pack (see below).

European Financial Stability Facility, European Stability Mechanism

The European Financial Stability Facility (EFSF) was set up in May 2010 as a temporary bail-out fund for the euro zone, used first for Greece. Its lending capacity was later raised to €440 billion. In 2012 it was replaced by a permanent European Stability Mechanism (ESM), based on an inter-governmental treaty, with a lending capacity initially of €500 billion.

Fiscal compact treaty

Formally known as the Treaty on Stability, Co-ordination and Governance in the Economic and Monetary Union, the fiscal compact was agreed in December 2011 and entered into force in January 2013.

The treaty commits signatories to amend national law to guarantee budget balance, defining this as keeping cyclically adjusted structural deficits below 0.5% of GDP. Because the UK and the Czech Republic refused to sign, the treaty was adopted as an inter-governmental one by 25 EU countries.

Six-pack, two-pack, Euro Plus Pact

Complementing the fiscal compact treaty are rules under the "excessive deficits procedure", agreed in 2011 and 2012. The six-pack refers to five regulations and a directive to control budget deficits and macroeconomic imbalances; the two-pack to provisions for the European Commission to monitor and if necessary require amendments to national budgets. The voting for sanctions is changed from positive to negative qualified majority: that is, it now takes a majority of countries to reject rather than approve proposals from the Commission. The Euro Plus Pact, signed by six other EU countries besides the euro zone, concerns broader economic co-ordination. Collectively these provisions are known as the "European semester".

Banking union

Negotiations on the details of banking union are continuing, but a single supervisory mechanism (SSM) has been set up and agreement has been reached on a single resolution mechanism (SRM). The first transfers supervision of the most important banks to the European Central Bank; the second sets out arrangements for managing a bank failure. These apply to euro-zone countries and other EU countries that choose to join (the UK, the Czech Republic and Sweden will not do so). The European Banking Authority continues to govern all banks in the EU.

Appendix 3
Further reading

Despite the euro's and the European Union's relative youth, there is a vast amount of literature on both. The footnotes to the text cite several sources that have been especially helpful. Below is a list of some books that readers might wish to consult.

Almqvist, K. and Linklater, A. (eds), *The Pursuit of Europe*, Axel and Margaret Axson Johnson Foundation, 2012

Authers, J., *Europe's Financial Crisis: A Short Guide to How the Euro Fell Into Crisis, and the Consequences for the World*, Pearson Education, 2013

Bastasin, C., *Saving Europe: How National Politics Nearly Destroyed the Euro*, Brookings Institutions Press, 2012

Booth, P. (ed.), *The Euro: the Beginning, the Middle ... and the End?*, IEA, 2013

Carswell, S., Anglo Republic, *Inside the Bank that Broke Ireland*, Penguin Ireland 2011

Cornelius, S., *Angela Merkel: The Authorised Biography*, Alma Books, 2013

Crawford, A. and Czuczka, T., *Angela Merkel: A Chancellorship Forged in Crisis*, Wiley, 2013

De Grauwe, P., *Economics of Monetary Union*, 9th edition, Oxford University Press, 2012

Gammelin, C. and Löw, R., *Europas Strippenzieher* (in German), Ullstein Buchverlage Berlin, 2014

Goulard, S. and Monti, M., *De la démocratie en Europe: Voir plus loin* (in French), Flammarion, 2012

Habermas, J., *The Crisis of the European Union: A Response*, Polity, 2012

Heise, M, *Emerging from the Europe Debt Crisis*, Springer, 2013

Hewitt, G., *The Lost Continent*, Hodder & Stoughton, 2013

Issing, O., *The Birth of the Euro*, Cambridge University Press, 2008

James, H., *Making the European Monetary Union*, Harvard University Press, 2012

Legrain, P., *European Spring: Why Our Economics and Politics are in a Mess – and How to Put Them Right*, CB Books (Amazon), 2014

Marsh, D., *Europe's Deadlock*, Yale University Press, 2013

Marsh, D., *The Euro: the Battle for a New Global Currency*, Yale University Press, updated 2011

O'Toole, F., *Ship of Fools: How Stupidity and Corruption Sank the Celtic Tiger*, Faber and Faber, 2009

Pisani-Ferry, J., *The Euro Crisis and its Aftermath*, Oxford University Press, 2014

Panagiotarea, E., *Greece in the Euro*, ECPR Press, 2013

Pryce, V., *Greekonomics*, Biteback, updated 2013

Soros, G., *The Tragedy of the European Union*, Public Affairs, 2014

Tsoukalis, L. and Emmanouilidis, J. (eds), *The Delphic Oracle on Europe*, Oxford University Press, 2011

Tsoukalis, L., *The Unhappy State of the European Union*, Policy Network, March 2014

Van Middelaar, L., *The Passage to Europe*, Yale University Press, 2013

Appendix 4

How *The Economist* saw it at the time

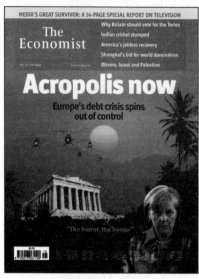

May 1st–7th 2010

July 10th–16th 2010

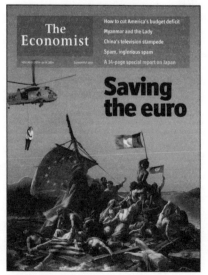

November 20th–26th 2010

December 4th–10th 2010

January 15th–21st 2011

March 12th–18th 2011

June 11th–17th 2011

June 25th–July 1st 2011

October 29th–November 4th 2011

November 5th–11th 2011

November 12th–18th 2011

November 26th–December 2nd 2011

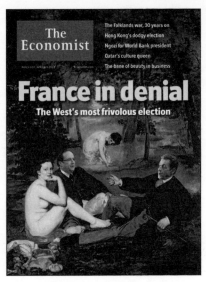

February 18th–24th 2012

March 31st–April 6th 2012

May 19th–25th 2012

May 26th–June 1st 2012

July 28th–August 3rd 2012

August 11th–17th 2012

November 17th–23rd 2012

March 23rd–29th 2013

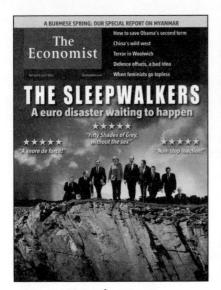

May 25th–31st 2013

September 14th–20th 2013

October 26th–November 1st 2013

January 4th–10th 2014

Index